The coloured boxes show the extents and page numbers for all maps in this Road Atlas.
The box colours correspond to the maps' page trim colours, representing different scales and types of map.

1:2,000,000 maps
Cover the entire region. Essential for long-distance road touring and route-planning.

1:1,000,000 maps
Cover southern and eastern South Africa, including Swaziland and Lesotho, at a scale ideal for journeys on and off the beaten track.

Feature maps
Areas of special interest shown in greater detail for in-depth exploration.

City maps
Everything you'll need to discover all the national capitals and major cities of the region.

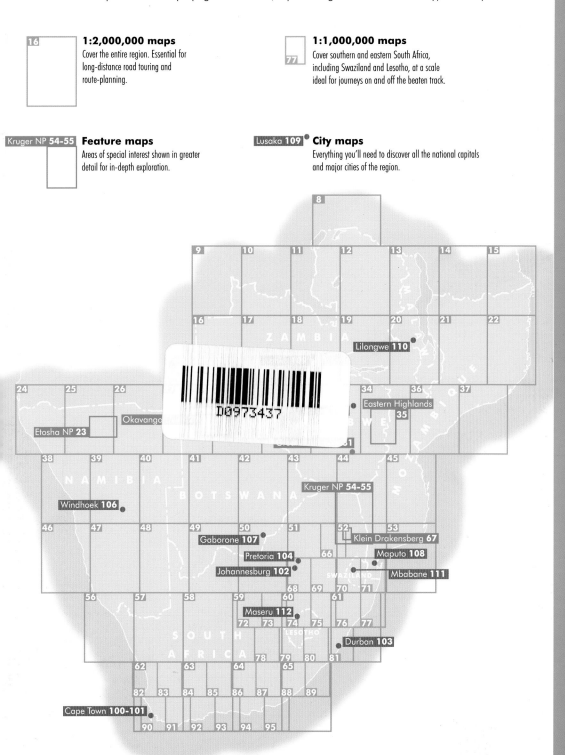

ELEVATION

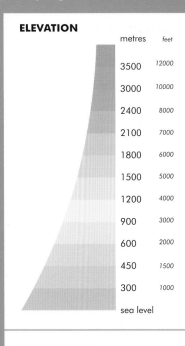

metres	feet
3500	12000
3000	10000
2400	8000
2100	7000
1800	6000
1500	5000
1200	4000
900	3000
600	2000
450	1500
300	1000
sea level	

BOUNDARIES

International Boundary
Limites Internationales
Straatsgrenze
Frontera Internacional

Provincial Boundary
Limites de la Province
Landesgrenze
Frontera de Provincia

National Park
Parc National
Nationalpark
Parque Nacional

Game Reserve, other park
Réserve Naturelle, autres parcs
Wildreservat, andere Parks
Reserva de Fauna, otros parques

Marine Park
Parc Maritime
Marine Park
Parque Marino

Military/Prohibited Area
Zone Militaire/Interdite
Militär-/Sperrgebiet
Zona Militar/Prohibida

Fence
Clôture
Zaun
Valla

TRANSPORTATION

Tollway
Autoroute à péage
gebührenpflichtige Autobahn
Autopista

Freeway
Autoroute
Autobahn
Autovía

Freeway under construction
Autoroute en construction
Autobahn in Bau
Autovía en construccion

Primary Road
Route Principale
Femstraße
Carretera Principal

Secondary Road
Route Secondaire
Nebenstraße
Carretera Secundaria

Other roads
Autres Routes
Übrige Straße
Otras Carreteras

Unsealed Roads
Route non bitumée
unversiegelte Straße
Carretera sin Asfaltar

4WD Track
Sentier
Fahrspur
Senda

 25 Distance in Kilometres
Distance en Kilomètres
Entfernung in Kilometern
Distancia en Kilómetros

Railway
Voie de chemin de fer
Eisenbahn
Ferrocarril

Ferry Route; Ferry Terminal
Route de ferry; Terminal du ferry
Fährroute; Fährnlegestelle
Transbordador; Estación Marítima

 Route Numbers
Numéro de Route
Straße Nummer
Número de Autopista

NATURAL FEATURES

River
Fleuve
Fluß
Rio

Creek, Irrigation Channel
Ruisseau; Canal d'irrigation
Flußarm; Bewässerungskanal
Riachuelo; Acequia

Intermittent River or Creek
Rivière, ruisseau intermittent
zeitweise wasserführender Fluß oder Bach
Río o Riachuelo Intermitente

Lake; Intermittent Lake
Lac; Lac intermittent
See; zeitweise wasserführender See
Lago; Lago Intermitente

 Waterfall; Rapids
Cascades; Rapides
Wasserfall; Stromschnellen
Catarata; Rápidos

Spring, Waterhole
Source, Mare
Quelle, Wasserloch
Manantial, Charco

Die Berg Mountain
Montagne
Berg
Montaña

Cliff
Falaise
Klippe, Steilabbruch
Acantilado

Swamp
Marais
Sumpf
Pantano

Salt Pans
Lac de sal
Salzpfanne
Salina

Reef
Récife
Riff
Arrecife

**For map features on the City Maps
in this Atlas (pp 100-112), please
refer to the City Map Legend p99.**

SYMBOLS

✈ ✚ **Airport; Airfield**	⊠ **Battle Site**
Aéroport; Aérodrome	Champ de Bataille
Flughafen; Flugplarz	Schlachtstelle
Aeropuerto; Pista de Aterrizaje	Campo de Batalla
Beach	🦩 **Bird Sanctuary**
Plage	Rèserve d'oiseaux
Strand	Vogelschutzgebiet
Playa	Reserva Ornitológica
◉ **Border Crossing**	⬛ **Camping Ground**
Frontières	Terrain de Camping
Grenzübergang	Zeltplatz
Cruce de Frontera	Camping
⌂ **Cave**	✚ **Church**
Grotte	Église
Höhle	Kirche
Cueva	Iglesia
Fort	⋈ **Gate**
Château Fort	Porte
Festung	Tor
Fuerte	Puerta
✿ **Gardens**	ℹ **Information Centre**
Jardins	Centre d'information
Gärten	Informationszentrum
Jardines	Centro de Información
🗼 **Lighthouse**	**Lodge, Safari Camp**
Phare	Pavillon, Campement
Leuchtturm	Jagdhütte, Safarilager
Faro	Pabellón de Caza, Campamento Safari
☼ **Lookout**	⊠ **Mine**
Point de Vue	Mine
Aussicht	Mine
Mirador	Mina
▲ **Monument**	**National Park**
Monument	Parc National
Denkmal	Nationalpark
Monumento	Parque Nacional
)(**Pass**	● **Point of Interest**
Col	Curiosités
Paß	Sehenswerter Ort
Desfiladero	Punto de Interés
✦ **Ruins**	**Toilet**
Ruines	Toilettes
Ruinen	Toiletten
Ruinas	Servicios
Walking Trail Base	🗼 **Windmill**
Piste du camp de base	Moulin à vent
Ausgangsbasis für Wanderpfad	Windmühle
Campamento base del trek	Molino

POPULATION

• Seshote	0 - 1,000
○ Gumare	1,000 - 5,000
○ Palapye	5,000 - 10,000
○ **Stellenbosch**	10,000 - 50,000
○ **Zomba**	50,000 - 100,000
○ **Kitwe**	100,000 - 250,000
○ **Beira**	250,000 - 500,000
○ **SOWETO**	> 500,000

✪ **Maputo** National Capital
Capitale Nationale
Hauptstadt
Capital Nacional

○ **Bisho** Provincial Capital
Capitale de Province
Landeshauptstadt
Capital de Provincia

Urban Area
Zone urbanisée
Stadtgebiet
Zona Urbana

USING THIS ROAD ATLAS

Okavango Delta, Map29

Extents of Larger Scale Map, with Page No.
Renvoi sur une carte à plus grande échelle
Ausdehnung von Karten größeren Maßstabs mit Seitenzahl
Extensiones de mapa a escala mayor con número de página

▲52▲

Adjoining Map Indicator
Repère indiquant la présence d'une carte adjacente
Anzeiger angrenzender Karten
Indicador de Mapa Colindante

No Adjoining Map
Pas de carte adjacente
keine angrenzende Karte
Sin Mapa Colindante

A   B   C   D

DEMOCRATIC REPUBLIC OF CONGO (ZAÏRE)

Lake Mweru

Ambrezete   Uige   Camabatela   Cassango   Cuilo   Andrada   Lucapa   Nchelenge   Kawambwac
Ambriz   N'Dalatando   Caombo   Lubalo   Saurimo   Sandoa   Kafakumba   Kashiba
Luanda   Caxito   Malanje   Xa Muteba   Cacolo   Muconda   Luau   Lubumbashi   Sam   Ma
Ponta das Palmeirinhas   Dondo   Calulo   Mussende   Quirima   Mwinilunga   Cazombo   Solwezi   Chililabombwe   Muf
Gabela   Andulo   Camacupa   Luena   Zambezi   Kabompo   North-Western   Chingola   Kitwe   Nc
Sumbe   Bailundo   Lucusse   Luanshya   Copperbell
Lobito   Balombo   **Kuito**   **ANGOLA**   Lumbala   Kabwe   Cen   **Lusa**
Benguela   **Huambo**   Chitembo   Cangamba   Chiumi   Mongu   Mumbwa   **ZAMBI**
Cubal   Caconda   Menongue   Kabwe   Lus
Lucira   Impulo   Capelongo   Cuito   Namwala   Mazabuka   Southern   Ka
Lubango   Cassinga   Caiundo   Mavinga   Senanga   Mulobezi   Choma   Lake Kariba
Namibe   Virei   Mulondo   Rio Cuando   Katima Mulilo   Livingstone   Kadc
Ponta Albina   Chiange   Savate   Muine   Kasane   Victoria Falls   Hwange   **ZIM**
Pediva   Otchinjau   N'Giva   Okavango River   Caprivi Strip Caprivi   Chobe   Lupane   Kwe Kv
Kunene River   Xangongo   Rundu   Gumare   Okavango Delta   Maun   **Bulawayo**   Gwe
Cape Fria   Oshikango   Ohangwena   Okavango   Ngamiland   Matabeleland   Gwan
Opuwo   **Oshakati**   Oshana   Otjikoto   Tsumeb   Grootfontein   Ghanzi   Orapa   North-East   Matabe South
Sesfontein   Etosha Pan   Otjozondjupa   Gaborone   Central
Etosha NP   Otavi   Omaheke   Serowe   Palapye   Beitor
Kamanjab   **BOTSWANA**   Francistown   North Provi
Khorixas   Ugab River   **Otjiwarongo**   Ghanzi   Pietersbu Polokwar
Cape Cross   Omaruru   Kalahari Desert   Ellisras   Polokwar
Erongo   Okahandja   Gobabis   Kweneng   Mochudi   Kgatleng   Pretori
Usakos   **Windhoek**   Ncojane   Khudumelapye   Molepole   **Gaborone**
Swakopmund   Khomas   Tshane   Kanye   Lobatse   Rustenburg   Gauteng
Pelican Point   **NAMIBIA**   Kgalagadi   Mmabatho   Mafikeng   **Johannesburg**   Vereenig
Walvis Bay   Hardap   Kalahari Desert   Southern   Klerksdorp   North-West   Vryburg   Standerton
Mariental   Tshabong   Province   Kroonstad   Bohlako
Maltahöhe   Hotazel   Vaal River   Thabong   Estco
Diaz Point   Karas   Kuruman   Free State   **Maseru**
Lüderitz   **Keetmanshoop**   Karasburg   Upington   **Kimberley**   **Bloemfontein**   **LESOTHO**
Namib Desert   Rosh Pinah   **SOUTH**   Springfontein   Aliwal North   Koks
ATLANTIC OCEAN   Alexander Bay   Vioolsdrif   Orange River   Prieska   Colesberg   Maclear   Umtata
Wreck Point   Pofadder   Kenhardt   **AFRICA**   Middelburg   Bisho   Pc
Kleinsee   Britstown   De Aar   Queenstown   St J   Eastern Cape
Hondeklipbaai   Kamieskroon   Brandvlei   Victoria West   Graaff-Reinet   Fort Beaufort   East Londo
Calvinia   Carnarvon   Somerset East   Grahamstown
Vredendal   Clanwilliam   Great Karoo   Beaufort West   Uitenhage   Port Alfred
Lambert's Bay   Citrusdal   Matjiesfontein   Oudtshoorn   **Port Elizabeth**
Saldanha   Western Cape   Worcester   George   Knysna   Cape St Francis
Malmesbury   Caledon   Mosselbaai
Cape Town   Simon's Town   Bredasdorp   Cape Agulhas
Cape of Good Hope

White boxes show map coverage at 1:2,000,000 scale.
See Map Locator (p1) for map coverage at larger scales.

10°E   15°E   20°E   25°E

10°S   15°S   20°S   25°S   30°S   35°S

0   200   400 km
0   100   200 mi

E   **F**   **G**   **H**

Bulaya
Mbala
Ilungu
porokoso
Tunduma
Kasama
Karonga
ba Northern
Chambeshi
ngweulu
Mpika
Mzuzu
Chipata
Eastern
Lilongwe
Songo
Zomba
Balaka
Tete
Blantyre
Nsanje
hoyi
Bindura
Harare
Quelimane
Mutare
Chimoio
Masvingo
Great
Zimbabwe
Beira
redzi
Divinhe
asvingo
Inhassoro
Massangena
Vilankulo
Gaza
Mabote
Chigubo
Thohoyandou
Pomene
Chókuè
Inhambane
Xai-Xai
spruit
Maputo
Mbabane
Louwsburg
SWAZILAND
St Lucia Resort
Empangeni
Gingindlovu
etermaritzburg
Durban
Umzinto
rt Shepstone

Dar es Salaam
Iringa
Utete
Mahenge
Kilwa Kivinje
TANZANIA
Liwale
Songea
Tunduru
Masasi
Mikindani
Quionga
Cabo Delgado
Moçimboa da Praia
Quiterajo
Mucojo
Ibo
Pemba
Lichinga
Niassa
Nantulo
Montepuez
Maúa
Namuno
Cuamba
Memba
Nampula
Nacala
Angoche
Moma
Pebane
Chinde
Ponta Timbue

COMOROS
Moroni Grand Comore
Anjouan
Mohéli
Mamoudzou
Mayotte
(Fr)
Antsiranana
Ambilobe
Andoany
Ambanja
Sambava
Bealanana
Antsohihy
Andapa
Antalaha
Mahajanga
Mandritsara
Tanjona
Vilanandro
Ambodifotatra
Andilamena
Maintirano
Tsiroanomandidy
Toamasina
Antananarivo
Antsirabe
Morondava
Ambositra
Mlandrivazo
MADAGASCAR
Fianarantsoa
Mananjary
Ihosy
Manakara
Morombe
Farafangana
Toliara
Vangaindrano
Taolagnaro
Ambovombe
Tanjona Vohimena

INDIAN
OCEAN

Mozambique Channel
Tropic of Capricorn
Bassas da India (Fr)
Île de l'Europa (Fr)

Distance is measured in kilometres and assumes travel on the most direct route using main roads and highways. See also Trip Maps on pages 96-98.

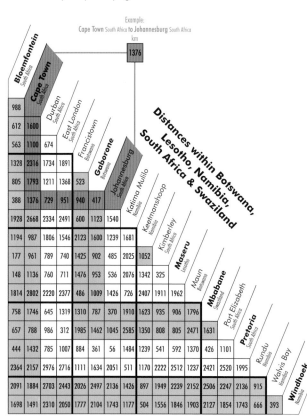

Example:
Cape Town South Africa **to** Johannesburg South Africa
km
1376

Mozambique Warning

Severe flooding in early 2000 inundated large areas of Maputo, Gaza Inhambane; parts of southern Sofala and Manica provinces were also aff ed. In the worst hit areas, roads were cut, bridges washed away, crops d aged, homes and buildings destroyed. Many coastal resorts also suffered d age. While it is likely that main roads will soon be passable again, travel should expect that secondary roads and bridges may not yet have be repaired, and road conditions may differ from those described here. Get update on conditions before setting your plans.

Driving in Southern Africa

The standard of driving in Southern Africa varies considerably and drivers be unpredictable. Be particularly careful in South Africa as there's a gre proportion of good roads and fast cars. In all the countries covered in atlas, traffic officially drives on the left - although you wouldn't always kn it. Be particularly prepared for blind corners and hills.

Road standards vary considerably from smooth highways to dirt tracks. most difficult to drive on are the tar roads full of bone-crunching pothole and in countries like Malawi, Zambia and Mozambique there are plenty these.

Tree branches on the road are the local version of warning triangles; the probably a broken-down vehicle ahead. Other things to be prepared for, e on busy highways, are children playing, people selling goods or drying see and cyclists on the wrong side of the road.

In rural areas, watch out for wildlife. Hitting even a small mammal damage a car considerably and hitting something large, like a kudu, can fatal for all concerned. Everywhere, watch for livestock. If you see children w red flags on the road, it means they're leading a herd of cows.

All of these things become much harder to deal with in the do Additionally, many vehicles have faulty lights - or none at all. It is stror recommended that you don't drive at night.

Driving off the Tar

Many roads in Southern Africa (even some main highways) are surfaced with gravel instead of tar. Some are well maintained, others aren't. Even on good gravel roads (deceptively easy to drive on) keep your speed below 100km/h. For long drives, lower your tyre pressure by about 25%. If the road is corrugated, gradually increase your speed until the vibrations stop - usually at about 65km/h.

Avoid swerving sharply or braking suddenly, and keep out of soft gravel on the verge - you may lose control. Try to follow the ruts made by other vehicles. Some roads are crossed by patches of sand. If you hit these at high speed, you can lose control. Likewise, if you enter a sudden corner too quickly, you'll carry straight on and end up in the ditch.

Switch on your headlights so you can be seen in dusty conditions. Overtaking is extremely dangerous because your view can be obscured by the dust from the car ahead. Flashing your headlights will indicate that you want to overtake. If someone behind you flashes their lights, move as far to the left as possible.

Take care in rainy conditions - gravel roads can turn to quagmires and dips may fill with water. If you're uncertain about the depth of the water, don't cross until it drains off.

Pans

Never drive on a pan unless you know exactly what you're doing. If you take a 4WD onto a pan, stick to the edges until you're sure it's dry. Even if the pan seems dry, it can still be wet underneath - vehicles can break through the crust and become irretrievably bogged. Foul-smelling salt can mean the pan is wet and potentially dangerous. If in doubt, follow the tracks of other drivers.

Distances within Malawi, Mozambique, Zambia & Zimbabwe

Beira (Mozambique)	Beitbridge (Zimbabwe)	Blantyre (Malawi)	Bulawayo (Zimbabwe)	Harare (Zimbabwe)	Kitwe (Zambia)	Lilongwe (Malawi)	Lusaka (Zambia)	Maputo (Mozambique)	Mongu (Zambia)	Mutare (Zimbabwe)	Mzuzu (Malawi)	Nampula (Mozambique)	Tete (Mozambique)	
809														Beitbridge
562	1194													Blantyre
791	322	1061												Bulawayo
551	565	629	432											Harare
1751	1402	1416	1269	837										Kitwe
862	1304	300	1171	739	1116									Lilongwe
1391	1042	1077	848	477	360	756								Lusaka
1179	881	1741	1203	1466	2666	1851	2306							Maputo
1870	1304	1683	982	1083	966	1362	606	2751						Mongu
288	521	678	503	263	1100	788	740	1203	1582					Mutare
1214	1656	652	1523	1091	1350	352	1108	2203	1714	1140				Mzuzu
871	1680	671	1662	1300	1972	856	1612	2050	2218	1159	1208			Nampula
570	938	256	805	373	1181	366	821	1485	1427	422	718	927		Tete
1227	758	1402	436	773	772	1168	412	1639	546	1036	1520	2073	1146	Victoria Falls

Summer runs from November to March/April and is generally hot and wet in the eastern and central parts of the region, humid on the east coast and relatively dry in the west. Winter, from May to July/August, is drier and cooler with snow on the high ground. The temperature and humidity starts to rise again in Spring, from August/September to October.

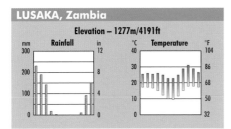

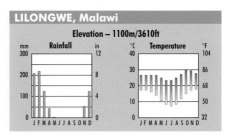

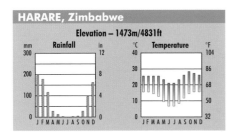

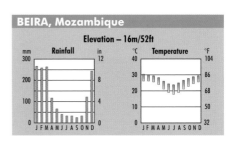

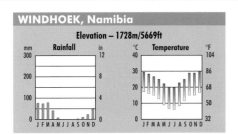

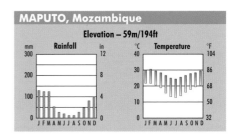

Tropical

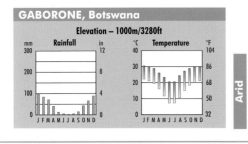

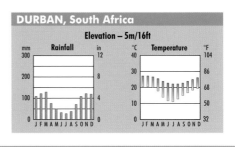

Arid

Sub-Tropical

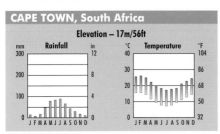

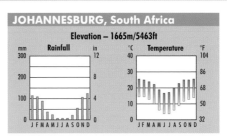

Temperate

Scale 1:2,000,000

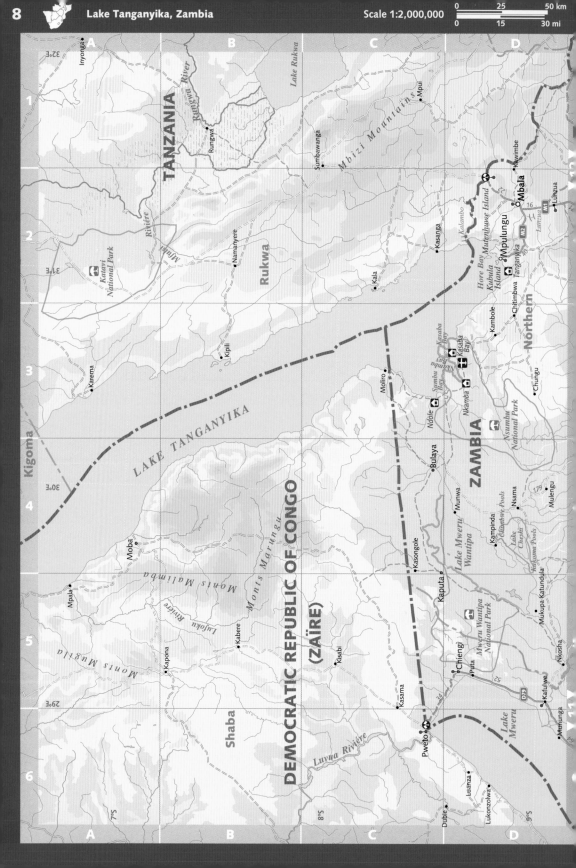

8

0　25　50 km
0　15　30 mi

TANZANIA

Rungwa River

Lake Rukwa

Inyonga

Rungwa

Namanyere

Rukwa

Katavi National Park

Mfuta Rivière

Mbizi Mountains

Sumbawanga

Mpui

Kasanga

Kala

Kalambo

Kambole

Mukenkuwe Island

Hore Bay

Kubula Island

Chitimbwa

Kawimbe

Mbala

Lunzua

Mpulungu

Tanganyika

Northern

Chungu

Kipili

Karema

Moliro

Kasaba Bay

Nkamba Bay

Sumbu Bay

Ndole

Bulaya

Nkamba

Nsumbu National Park

ZAMBIA

Chishet

Kigoma

LAKE TANGANYIKA

Monts Marungu

DEMOCRATIC REPUBLIC OF CONGO

(ZAÏRE)

Munwa

Kasongole

Lake Mweru Wantipa

Kaputa

Kampinda

Nsama

Chishet Pools

Kikoma Pools

Mulengu

179

Moba

Monts Malimba

Lufuku Rivière

Kabere

Mpala

Kapona

Monts Mugila

Kisabi

Kasama

Chiengi

Puta

Mweru Wantipa National Park

Mukupa Katundula

Nkosha

Kafulwe

D79

52

Lake Mweru

Munkunga

Shaba

Luvua Rivière

Pweto

Dubie

Lwanza

Lukonzolwa

7°S

8°S

9°S

29°E

30°E

31°E

32°E

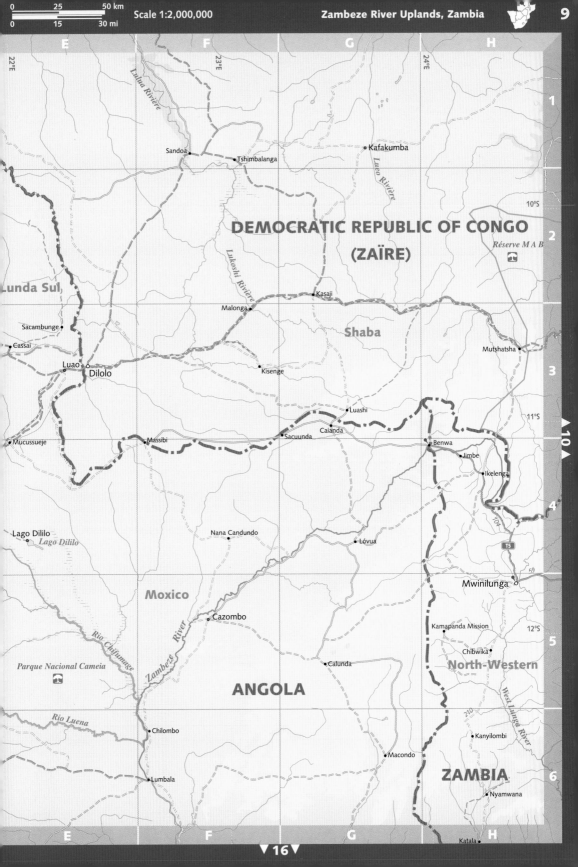

0   25   50 km
0   15   30 mi

22°E

E   F   G   H

1

Sandoa
Tshimbalanga
Kafakumba

Lulua Rivière

Lueo Rivière

23°E

24°E

10°S

**DEMOCRATIC REPUBLIC OF CONGO
(ZAÏRE)**

2

Réserve M A B

Lunda Sul

Lukoshi Rivière

Kasaji
Malonga

Shaba

Mutshatsha

Sacambunge
Cassai

Luao
Dilolo

Kisenge

3

11°S

Luashi
Caianda
Sacuunda
Massibi

Benwa
Jimbe
Ikelenga

Mucussueje

10

Lago Dililo
Lago Dililo

Nana Candundo

Lóvua

T4

4

T5

59

Mwinilunga

Moxico

Cazombo

Rio Chifumage

Zambeze River

Kamapanda Mission

Chibwika

12°S

5

Parque Nacional Cameia

Calunda

North-Western

ANGOLA

West Lunga River

Rio Luena

Chilombo

Kanyilombi

270

ZAMBIA

Lumbala

Macondo

6

Nyamwana

E   F   G   H

Katala

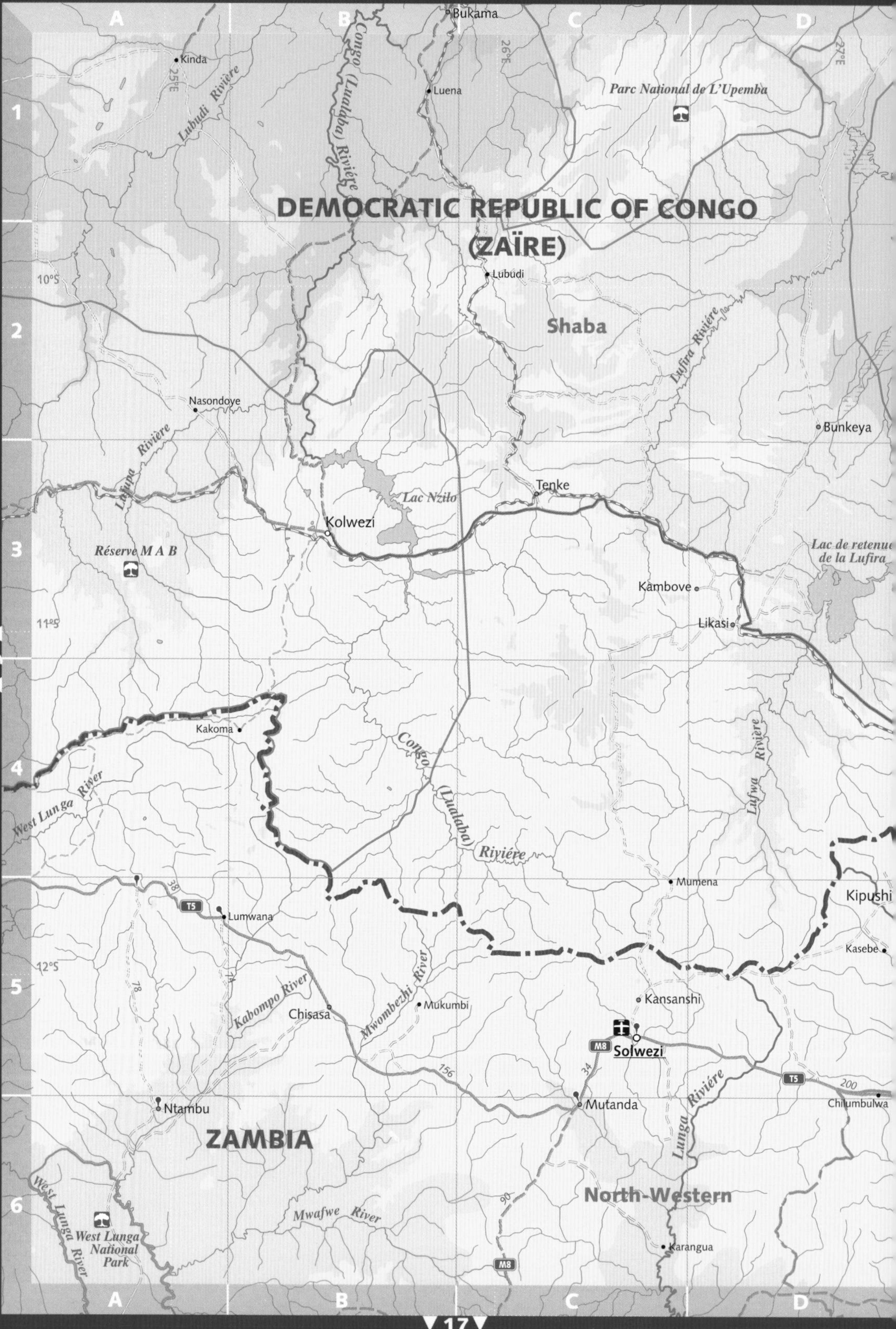

DEMOCRATIC REPUBLIC OF CONGO
(ZAÏRE)
Bukama
Kinda
Luena
Lubudi Rivière
Congo (Lualaba) Rivière
Parc National de L'Upemba
Lubudi
Shaba
Lufira Rivière
Nasondoye
Bunkeya
Lufupa Rivière
Lac Nzilo
Tenke
Kolwezi
Réserve M A B
Lac de retenue de la Lufira
Kambove
Likasi
Kakoma
Congo (Lualaba) Rivière
Lufwa Rivière
West Lunga River
Mumena
Kipushi
Lumwana
Kasebe
Kabompo River
Chisasa
Mwombezhi River
Mukumbi
Kansanshi
Solwezi
Mutanda
Lunga Rivière
Chilumbulwa
Ntambu
ZAMBIA
North-Western
West Lunga River
Mwafwe River
West Lunga National Park
Karangua
10°S
11°S
12°S
25°E
26°E
27°E
A
B
C
D
1
2
3
4
5
6
9
17

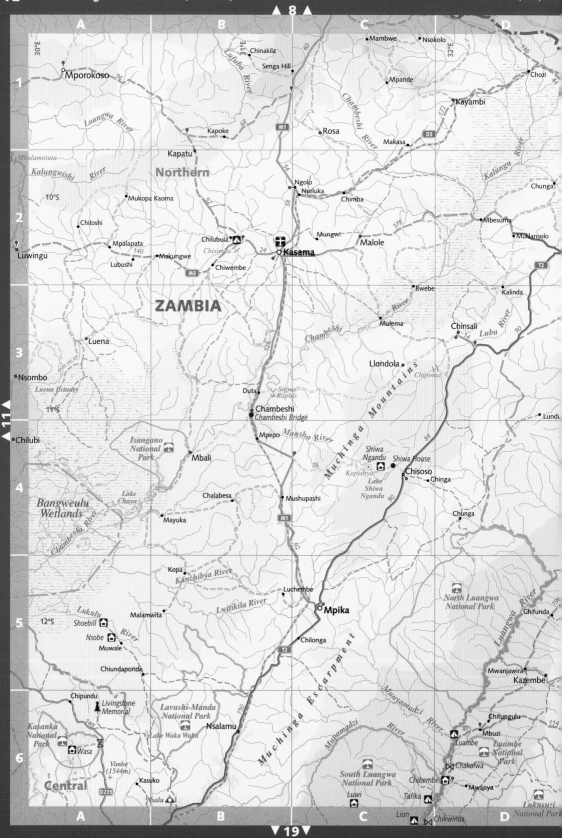

Mporokoso

Chinakila

Senga Hill

Mambwe Nsokolo

Mpande

Chozi

Kayambi

Kapoke

Kapatu

Rosa

Makasa

Northern

Ngolo
Nseluka

Chimba

Chunga

Mukopa Kaoma

Chitoshi

Mpalapata

Chilubula

Mungwi

Malole

Mbesuma

Muilansolo

Luwingu

Lubushi

Makungwe

Chiwembe

Kasama

ZAMBIA

Bwebe

Kalinda

Mulema

Chinsali

Luena

Llondola

Nsombo

Luena Estuary

Duta

Chambeshi
Chambeshi Bridge

Chilubi

Mpepo

Isangano
National
Park

Mbali

Shiwa
Ngandu

Shiwa House

Chisoso

Chinga

Kapishya

Lake
Shiwa
Ngandu

Lundu

Chalabesa

Mushupashi

Bangweulu
Wetlands

Lake
Chaya

Mayuka

Chunga

Kopa

Kanchibya River

Luchembe

North Luangwa
National Park

Chifunda

Lwitikila River

Malamwita

Lukulu

Shoebill

Nsobe

Muwale

Mpika

Mwanjawira

Kazembe

Chilonga

Chiundaponde

Chipundu

Livingstone
Memorial

Lavushi-Manda
National Park

Nsalamu

Muchinga Escarpment

Chitungulu

Mbuzi

Luambe

Luambe
National
Park

Kasanka
National
Park

Wasa

Vimbe
(1544m)

Lake Waka Waka

Kasuko

Central

Nsalu

South Luangwa
National Park

Luwi

Chibembe

Chakolwa

Mwanya

Tafika

Lukusuzi
National
Park

Lion

Chikwinda

0   25   50 km
0   15   30 mi

TANZANIA

Kipengere Range
Mbeya

Vwawa
Mbozi
Mwenzo Mission
Tunduma
Nakonde
Nyala
Chitipa
Chisenga
Kampumbu
Malabi
Muyombe
Katumbi
Chama
Tembwe
Mbeya
Chikwa
Lundazi
Kavinga

Mt Rungwe (2961m)
Tukuyu
Ipinda
Matema
Ikombe
Lumbila
Songwe River Bridge
Ibanda
Kyela
Itungi
Songwe
Kambwe
Kaporo
Karonga
Mdandu
Njombe
Iringa
Lisitu
Lukumburu
Milo
Lupingo
Cape Kaiser
Rudewa

Makuta Mountains

Mulale Bay
Ngara
Mt Mpanda (2017m)
Nthalire
Nyika National Park
Nganda Peak (2607m)
Kaperekezi
Chelinda
Mt Ntakati (2503m)
Nyika Plateau
Kaziwiziwi
Livingstonia
Haniniya
Thazima
Juniper Forest
Lura
Mt Mtumbi (2627m)
Chiweta
Ruruku Point
Nchenachena
Muhuju
Mwazisi
Ng'onga
Bolero
Rumphi
Bwengu

LAKE
Chilumba
Chitimba
Ameliz Bay
Young's Bay
Manda
Lituhi
Ndombi Bay
Ruhuhu River
Rūvuma
Mango
Mbinga
Ruvuma River
Tumbi Point
Liuli
Mpepaya

Vwaza Wildlife Reserve
Vwaza Marsh
Kazuni
Lake Kazuni
Kazuni
MALAWI
Ruarwe
Usisya Bay
Usisya
Mphandi Point
Dankhoyo Bay
Cape Manulo
Chikwina
Kandoli Mountains
Lukoma Bay
Mbamba Bay

Enuckweni
Ekwendeni
Kafukule
Mzuzu
Chikwa
Mbeya
Northern
Mt Mpamphala (1954m)
Mukwiya
Nkhata Bay
Nkhata Bay
Chizi Point
Songa Point
Mitomani
Lupilichi
Monte Txitonga (1848m)

Chikangawa
Mzimba
Viphya Forest Reserve
Kasito Luweya River
Viphya Plateau
Chintheche
Bandawe
Bandawe Point
MALAWI
Likoma Island
Chizimulu Island
Cóbuè

Eastern
Edingeni
Luwawa Forest
Lundazi
Jenda
Katete
Unaka Lagoon
MOZAMBIQUE
Manda Wilderness Area
Niassa
Sanga
Sanga Reserve
Macaloge

Dwangwa
Central
Nkhotakota Wildlife Reserve
Metangula
Nova Coimbra
Messumba
Macalibугua

Songwe River
Songwe
Luangwa River
North Rukuru River
Rukuru River
Luwumbu River
South Bukura River
Kasitu River
Luweya River
Lundazi River
Dwangwa River
Lunho Rio
Rio Messinge
Rio Msuula
Rio Molibango
Planalto de Lichinga

M9
M26
M1
M9
M1
M5
M110

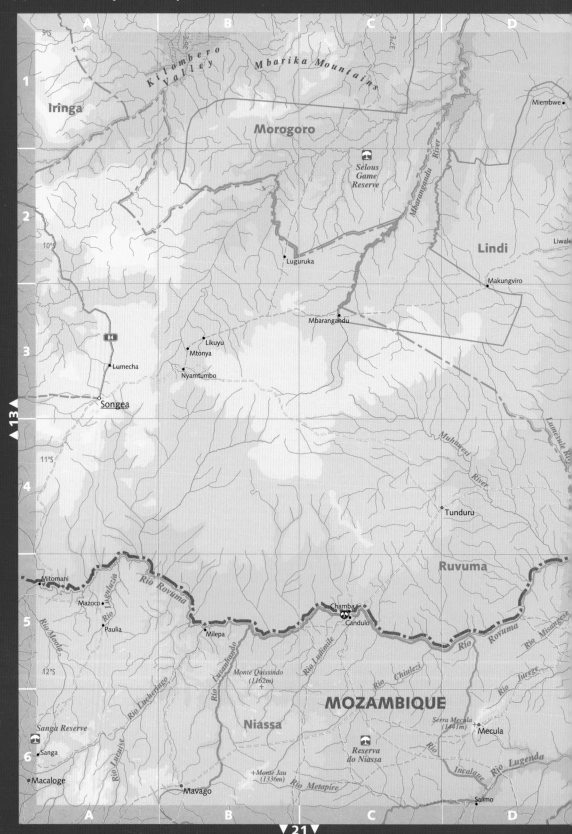

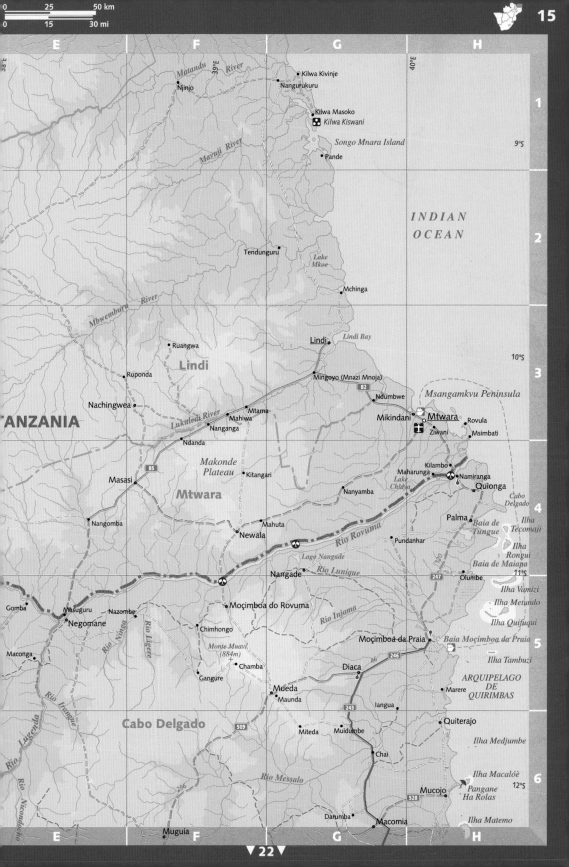

0   25   50 km
0   15   30 mi

E   **F**   **G**   **H**

Matandu River   39°E

Njinjo

Kilwa Kivinje
Nangurukuru

1

Kilwa Masoko
Kilwa Kiswani

Mavuji River

Pande

Songo Mnara Island

9°S

I N D I A N

O C E A N

2

Tendunguru

Lake
Mkoe

Mbwembura River

Mchinga

Ruangwa

Lindi

Lindi Bay

Lindi

10°S

3

Ruponda

Mingoyo (Mnazi Mnoja)

R2

Ndumbwe

Msangamkvu Peninsula

Nachingwea

Lukuledi River

Mtama

Mahiwa

Mikindani   **Mtwara**

Rovula

TANZANIA

Nanganga

Ziwani

Msimbati

Ndanda

Makonde
Plateau

Kitangari

Kilambo

Maharunga

Namiranga

Masasi

85

Lake
Chidya

Quionga

Mtwara

Nanyamba

Cabo
Delgado

4

Nangomba

Mahuta

Palma

Baia de
Tungue

Ilha
Tecomaji

Newala

Rio Rovuma

Pundanhar

Ilha
Rongui
Baia de Maiapa

Lago Nangade

Rio Lunique

Olumbe

11°S

Nangade

R30

Ilha Vamizi

Ilha Metundo

Moçimboa do Rovuma

Rio Injama

Ilha Quifuqui

Gomba

Nazombe

Ilha
Ligere

Moçimboa da Praia

Baia Moçimboa da Praia

5

Masuguru

Chimhongo

Negomane

Rio Ninga

R247

Ilha Tambuzi

Maconga

Rio Ligere

Monte Muavi
(884m)

Chamba

Diaca

R246

Marere

ARQUIPELAGO
DE
QUIRIMBAS

Gangure

Mueda

Iangua

Rio Trangue

Maunda

R243

Quiterajo

Cabo Delgado

R509

Miteda

Muidumbe

Ilha Medjumbe

Rio Messalo

Chai

Ilha Macalóè

Rio Nicondecho

R256

Mucojo

Pangane
Ha Rolas

12°S

6

R528

Ilha Matemo

Muguia

Darumba

Macomia

E   **F**   **G**   **H**

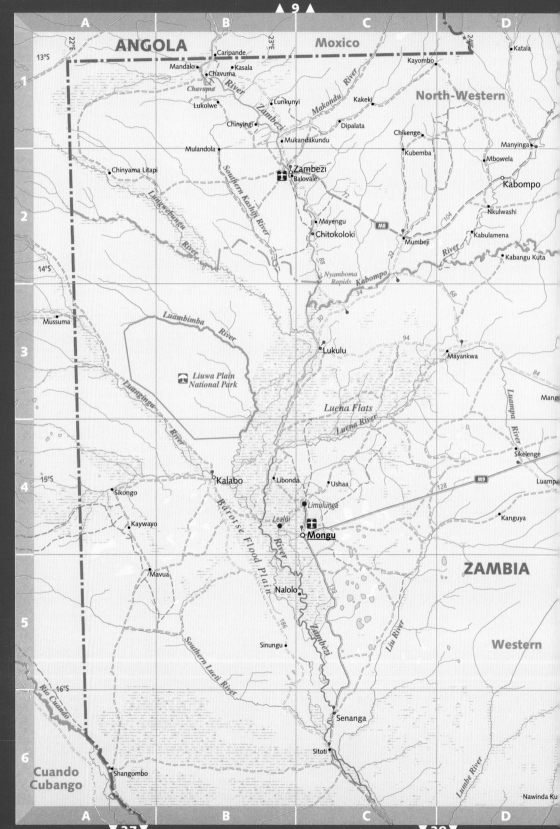

▲ 9 ▲

ANGOLA   Moxico

North-Western

Caripande

Mandalo
Chavuma
Kasala

Lukolwe
Chinyingi
Chinyama Litapi

Mulandola

Lunkunyi
Mukandakundu

Kayombo
Katala

Kakeki
Dipalata

Chikenge
Kubemba

Manyinga
Mbowela

Zambezi
Balovale

Kabompo

Mayengu
Chitokoloki

Mumbeji

Nkulwashi

Kabulamena
Kabangu Kuta

Mussuma

Luambimba River

Liuwa Plain
National Park

Lukulu

Mayankwa

Luena Flats

Luena River

Sikelenge

Kalabo

Sikongo

Kaywayo

Libonda
Ushaa

Limulunga

Lealui
Mongu

Kanguya

ZAMBIA

Mavua

Nalolo

Western

Sinungu

Barotse Flood Plain

Senanga

Sitoti

**Cuando
Cubango**

Shangombo

Nawinda

Nyamboma Rapids

Kabompo

M8

M9

Rio Cuando

▼ 27 ▼   ▼ 28 ▼

Scale:
0 — 25 — 50 km
0 — 15 — 30 mi

E | F | G | H

1

St Mary's
13°S

West Lunga
National Park

Mutumbwe

144

M8

Kawana

12

Ingwe

264

Kelongwa

Copperbelt

2

Kalengwa

Kasempa

26°E

Lunga Rivière

Kasompe

Dongwe River

Lufupa River

185

Ngabwe

14°S

234

Mushima

Busanga
Plains

Shumba

Kabanga

Lunga River

Kafue River

3

Ntemwa

Moshi

Hippo

Lubungu

Kaindu

Lalafuta River

26

Kaoma

Luena River

201

Tatayoyo

Lufupa

Kafwala

Kafue National Park

Kafue River

94

Kaporoso

▲ 18 ▲

4

Mayukweyukwe
Rapids

M9

Park HQ

Mukambi Safari

Chunga Safari

63

Natusanga

15°S

114

Mumbwa

Kungulu

Kasula

Central

Liuwampa River

Puku Pan

Mwengwa
Rapids

115

30

Kapanda

5

Liyunyi Kuta

148

Katobo

D769

Lake
Itezhi-Tezhi

Itezhi-Tezhi
Dam

Kafue

River

Kafue
Flats

Blue Lagoon
National Park

Chunga
Lagoon

Ranger Post

Kafue National Park

Musungwa

Itezhitezhi

New Kalala

40

Namwala

Kantengwa

Lochinvar
National Park

Park
HQ

16°S

Kabulamwanda

Chitongo

Park Gate

Kataba

Nanzhila River

Southern

Chongo

6

110

Nanzhila

M11

106

Chilala

Macha

Magunza

64

62

Pemba

Bilili Hot
Springs

E | F | G | H

T1

▲ 11 ▲

Kitwe

Saint Mary's

13°S

28°E

Old Slave Tree

Ndola

Bwana Mkubwa

DEMOCRATIC REPUBLIC OF CONGO (ZAÏRE)

Demalisques de Leshwe

Kan

29°E

Luanshya

1

Copperbelt

Kafulafuta

Pukota

Chilobia

Kafue River

Ibenga

Munkumpu

Saint Anthonys

Mpongwe

Walamba

Miengwe

Musofu

Mkushi River (Cha

108

Ndab

Kashitu

Mkushi Boma

2

Kangondi

14°S

Ngabwe

Mwinuama

Mukubwe

Tonde

96

Mpulo

Fiwila

Mulungwe

Shamputa

Kapiri Mposhi

Mkushi River

ZAMBIA

Kafue River

Central

Chipepo

Chibwe

Mita Hills Dam

Old Mkushi

Mboshya

3

Lukanga Swamp

Kabwe

Kampumba

Lunsemfwa

Lunsemfwa

Wonder Gorge

Luangenfwa River

Chitanda

Chibombo

Nyama

Mulungushi Dam

Malambanyama

Chikonkomene

Mulungushi

114

Landless Corner

Chisamba Safari

Chisamba

15°S

Fringilla Farm

Karubwe

Kasula

4

Mukulaikwa

Nakachenje

Kasisi

Lusaka International

Chongwe

Mwembeshi

Westwood

162

Rufunsa

Mukunku

Rufunsa River

Lusaka

Mwambashi River

Kapanda

Lusaka

Shishengula

Lower Zambezi National Park

Blue Lagoon National Park

Lilayi

Chilanga

Shapolao

Mpasi

Chongwe River

Mushika

Mpa Gorg

Kafue Flats

Sokola

Sausage Tree

Mwambashi River

Chewore

5

Nega Nega

Kafue

Royal Zambezi

Chongwe

Chiawa

Chikwenya

Lubompo

Kafue Gorge

Kayila

Chongwe Park Gate

Nyamepi

Sapi Safari Area

Mazabuka

Mugoto

Chapanga

Mana Pools

Chewore Safari Ar

Park Headquarters

Magoye

Kafue River

Gwabi

Chiawa

Mana Pools National Park

16°S

Park Gate

Kembe

Chirundu

Hurungwe Safari Area

Nyakasanga River

Manganyai

Escarpme

Chongo

Chiuuna

Changa

A1

Zambezi

Chitake Springs

Kamara

Chitanga

Monze

Kariba Gorge

Chipandahouri River

Gota Gota (1291m)

Toswe River

Chimakungwa (1240m)

Marongora

Mvlove

Ambakwe

Rukomechi River

Angw

6

Chisekesi

Zambezi River

Kuburi Wilderness Area

Chipitani

Makuti

Mashonaland West

Pemba

Gwembe

Siavonga

Kariba

Lake Kariba

Kariba Dam

Charara Safari Area

Chitomai

Vuti

Chivutsisigo

Makore

A   B   C   D

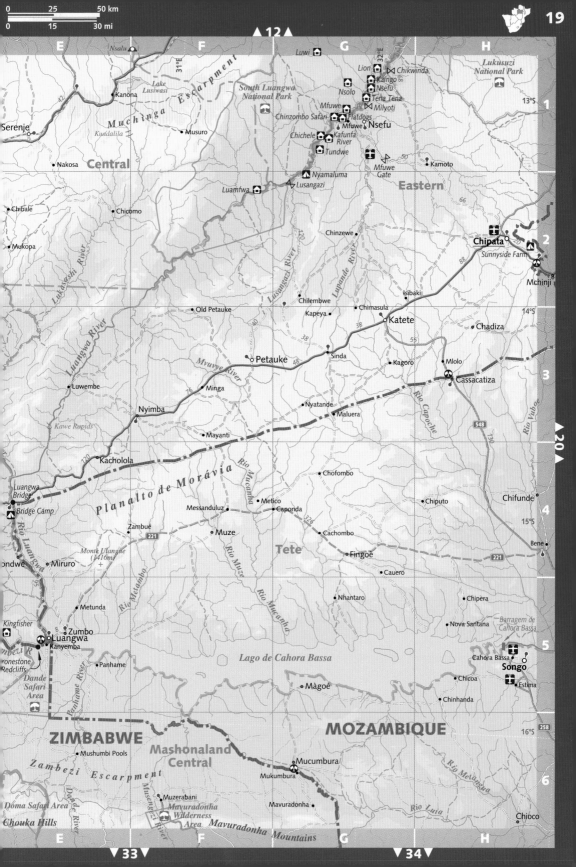

0   25   50 km
0   15   30 mi

E   **F**   **G**   **H**

Nsalu

Luwi

Lion

Chikwinda

Lukusuzi
National Park

Kanona

Lake
Lusiwasi

South Luangwa
National Park

Kaingo
Nsefu

Nsolo

Tena Tena
Milyoti

13°S **1**

Serenje

Muchinga

Kuadalila

Musuro

Mfuwe

Chinzombo Safari

Flatdogs
Mfuwe

Nsefu

Chibale

Chicomo

Chichele

Kafunfa
River

Central

Nakosa

Tundwe

Mfuwe
Gate

Kamoto

Mukopa

Eastern

Nyamaluma

Luamfwa

Lusangazi

66

Chinzewe

Chipata

Sunnyside Farm

Mchinji **2**

Chilembwe

Isibaki

Old Petauke

Kapeya

Chimasula

Katete

14°S

Chadiza

Kacholola

Luwembe

Myuvye River

Petauke

Sinda

Kagoro

Mlolo

Cassacatiza **3**

Minga

Nyatande

Maluera

Rio Capoche

▲ 20 ▲

Nyimba

Kawe Rapids

Mayanti

Chofombo

Chiputo

Chifunde

Luangwa
Bridge

Planalto de Morávia

Messanduluz

Metico

Caponda

Cachombo

15°S **4**

Bridge Camp

Zambué

Muze

Tete

Fingoè

Bene

Miruro

Monte Ulangue
(1416m)

Cauero

Metunda

Nhantaro

Chipera

Kingfisher

Zumbo

Luangwa

Nova Santana

Barragem de
Cahora Bassa

Cahora Bassa

Songo **5**

Kanyemba

Ironestone
Redcliffs

Panhame

Lago de Cahora Bassa

Màgoè

Chicoa

Estima

Dande
Safari
Area

Chinhanda

ZIMBABWE

**Mashonaland
Central**

Mucumbura

16°S

Chioco **6**

Mushumbi Pools

Mukumbura

Zambezi Escarpment

Doma Safari
Area

Muzerabani

Mavuradonha
Wilderness
Area

Mavuradonha

Rio Luia

Chouka Hills

Mavuradonha Mountains

Rio Metangua

E   **F**   **G**   **H**

MOZAMBIQUE

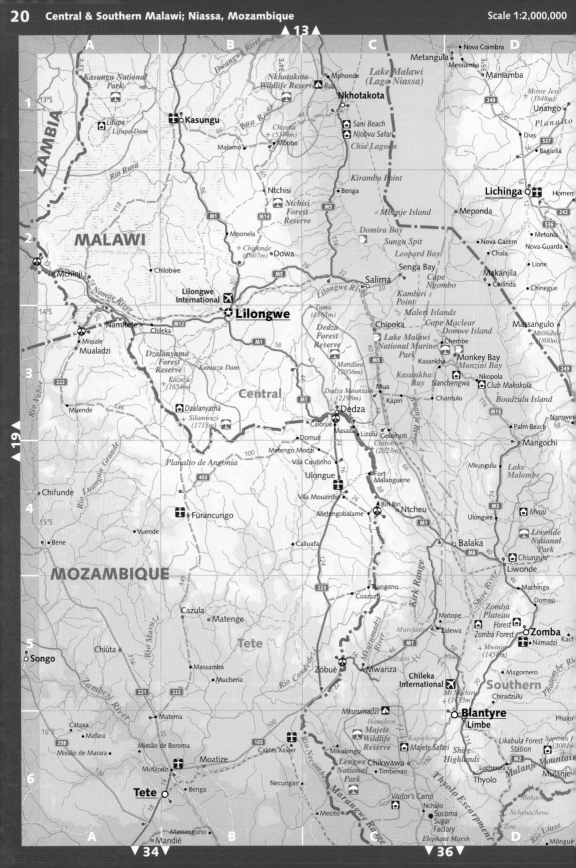

▲**13**▲

A   **B**   **C**   **D**

33°E

13°S

Kasungu National Park

Lifupa Lifupa Dam

ZAMBIA

Kasungu

66

Rio Rusa

118

96

Bua River

Dwangwa River

Nkhotakota Wildlife Reserve   Bua

Mphonde

Nkhotakota

Chipata (5174m)

Malomo   Mbbbo

44

Sani Beach

Njobvu Safari

Chia Lagoon

Lake Malawi (Lago Niassa)

Metangula   Messumba   Nova Coimbra

Maniamba

249

Monte Jesi (1848m)

Unango

Planalto

Dias

537

Bagarlia

Lichinga   Homen

242

MALAWI

Ntchisi

Ntchisi Forest Reserve

M1

M14

65

Benga

Kirambu Point

Mbenje Island

Meponda

536

Metonia

Nova Guarda

Mchinji

32

Chilobwe

Mponela

Chifonde (1607m)   Dowa

30

M5

78

Domira Bay

Sungu Spit

Leopard Bay

Salima

20

Senga Bay

Cape Ngombo

Kambiri Point

Nova Cacem   Chala

Makanjila   Chilinda

Lione   Chinegue

14°S

Namite River

M12

Chileka

Namitete

Lilongwe International   **Lilongwe**

M1   58

Lilongwe River

Tuma (4561m)

Chipoka

Malen Islands

Cape Maclear   *Domwe Island*

Massangulo

Msondole (1800m)

249

Rio Vúbue

222

Missale   Mualadzi

118

20

Dzalanyama Forest Reserve

Kazuzu (1654m)   *Kamuzu Dam*

136

Central

M1

42

Dedza Forest Reserve

Mundini (2056m)

M5

Lake Malawi National Marine Park

Chembe   Kasankha

Kasankha Bay

Monkey Bay

Manzini Bay

Nanchengwa   Nkopola

Chantulo   Club Makokola

Boadzulu Island

M15

Namwe

▲**19**▲

Muende

Dzalanyama   Silamwezi (1713m)

44

Dedza Mountain (2198m)

Dedza

Caloruè   Masasa

Mua   Kapiri

Lizulu   Golomoti

Chirobwe (2023m)

Palm Beach

58

Mangochi

15°S

MOZAMBIQUE

Chifunde

Rio Luangwa Grande

Planalto de Angonia

403

Domue

Metengo Modzi

Vila Coutinho

100

Ulongue

16

Vila Mouzinho

26

Fort Malanguene

88

Biri Biri   **Ntcheu**

Metengobalame

Mkungulu

Lake Malombe

74

Ulongwe

M3

Mvuu

M1

Liwonde National Park

Chiunguni

Furancungo

Caliuafa

Balaka

M8

40

Liwonde

46

Machinga

Rio Mavuzi

Cazula

Matenge

Tete

223

Tsangano   Cuazuzo

124

Kirk Range

Domasi

Zomba Plateau

Forest

Zomba Forest

Matope   Zalewa

Murchison

Shire River

M1

Namadzi   **Zomba**   Kach

Songo

Chiúta

Zambezi River

221

222

Massamba

Muchena

100

Zóbuè   Mwanza

Mkurumadzi River

Ndzani River

Nkula

Mwinie (1451m)

Magornero

Southern

70

Chileka International   *Mt Michiru (1173m)*

Chiradzulu

Phalor

258

Cataxa

Mafara

Missão de Marara

16

Zambezi River

30

Matema

Missão de Boroma

Moatize

103

Caldas Xavier

Rio Necomble

Mikolongo

Lengwe National Park

Majete Wildlife Reserve

Chikwawa

Timbenao

Mkurumadzi

Hamilton

Majete Safari

Shire Highlands

Kapichira

Nchalo   *Sucoma Sugar Factory*

Likabula Forest Station

(3001m)

M2

Luchenza

Thyolo

Mulanje Mountain

Mulanje

Blantyre

Limbe

Thyolo Escarpment

Sopinha Ri

Rio Liase

Mutando

Benga

Tete

18

Marangwe Range

Visitor's Camp

Nchalo

Elephant Marsh

Massangano

Mandié

Necungas

Mecito

Nchenachena

Makach

Zoa

Môngué

A   **B**   **C**   **D**

▼**34**▼   ▼**36**▼

0 25 50 km
0 15 30 mi

MOZAMBIQUE

14

Rio Metapire

Reserva do Niassa

Salimo

Mataca

Lichinga

Chiconono

Nanlixa

Monte Mecuia
+ (1738m)

Nova Viseu

Lumiar

13°S

Niassa

Litunde

Marrupa

Rio Lugenda

Rio Lureco

Rio Messalo

Majune

Malanga

Rèvia

242

248

Nungo

242

Nova Santarém

Muoco Muapula Vahiua

Catur

Rio Messalala

Rio Luchimua

Máua

Rio Rarunang

Nipepe

14°S

Mitande

Congerenge

8

Namicunde

Vatiua

Rio Lúrio

22

Metarica

Rio Luleio

Mecunica

Umpilua

Lalaua

Lago Amaramba

Nacumua

Mepica

Macallia

Namacala

Lake
Chiuta

Nampula

Nayuchi Entre Lagos

Rio Muenda

Cuamba

Lúrio

Mutuáli

Rio Lalaua

Rio Menatuti

Monte Mepalue
(1777m) +

Mecanhelas

Malema

8

Ribáuè

15°S

Chamba

231

Lioma

Iapala

Ribáuè Garè

104

Matucuta

Monte Namuli
+ (2419m)

Inago

Siquirir

Molumbo

Gurúè

Nauela

Vacha

Alto Ligonha

Nanraha

Planalto Moçambicano

Rio Luo

Socone

Alto Molócuè

232

Zambezia

Rio Munduzi

Namarrói

Muabarama

Naiopué

Mutala

Milange

Lipale

Erego

231

Mugulama

Rio Molócuè

Chá Lugela

Vulalo

Nipiodi

Uape

Mamala

Limbuè

Monte Mubu
(1710m) +

Mucúbi

Rio Meleia

Gilé

16°S

Chá Madal

Tacuane

36

37

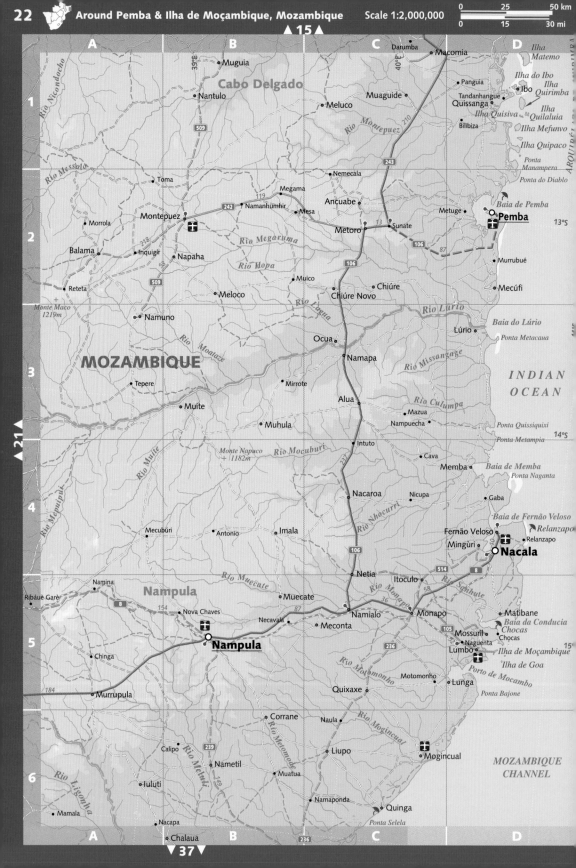

▲ **15** ▲

Cabo Delgado

Muguia

Nantulo

Ilha
Matemo

Ilha do Ibo   Ilha
                Quirimba
Panguia   Ibo
Tandanhangue
Quissanga   Ilha Quisiva   Ilha
                            Quilaluia
Bilibiza   Ilha Mefunvo

Ilha Quipaco

Meluco

Muaguide

Rio Nicondacho

509

Toma

Rio Messalo

Megama

Nemecala

Ancuabe

Ponta Manampera

Ponta do Diablo

119

242   Namanhumhir
Mesa

Metoro   Sunate

13

Metuge

Baia de Pemba

⚓ **Pemba**   13°S

Montepuez ✝

Morrola

218   Inquigir   Napaha

Rio Megaruma

Rio Hopa

106

87

106

Murrubué

Balama

509   Reteta

Meloco

Muico

Chiúre Novo   Chiúre

Rio Lúrio

Mecúfi

Monte Maco
1219m

Namuno

Rio Moataze

Rio Lugua

Rio Lúrio

Lúrio   Baia do Lúrio
        Ponta Metacaua

MOZAMBIQUE

Tepere

Ocua

Namapa

Mirrote

Rio Missangage

Rio Culumpa

**INDIAN
OCEAN**

Muite

Alua

Mazua

Ponta Quissiquixi

Muhula

Nampuecha   Ponta Metampia   14°S

Monte Napuco
+ 1182m

Rio Mocuburi

Intuto

Rio Muite

237

Cava

Memba   Baia de Memba
        Ponta Naganta

Rio Menupuki

Nacaroa

Nicupa

Gaba

Rio Nhocurri

Baia de Fernão Veloso

Fernão Veloso   ⤒ Relanzapo

Mecubúri   Antonio   Imala

Mingùri   Relanzapo

106

⚓ **Nacala**

Netia   Itoculo

514   8

Ribáué Garè

Namina

Nampula

Rio Muecate

Rio Monapo   58

Rio Senhute

8   154   Nova Chaves

Necavala   Muecate   87

Namialo   Monapo

36

Matibane

Baia da Conducia
Chocas

Meconta

105

Mossuril
Naguenta   Chocas

Chinga

⚓ **Nampula**

Rio Motomonho

236

Motomonho

Lumbo   Ilha de Moçambique

Ilha de Goa

Murrupula

Quixaxe   Lunga

Porto de Mocambo
Ponta Bajone

184

Corrane   Naula   Rio Mogincual

Calipo   239

Nametil   149

Liupo

⚓ Mogincual

**MOZAMBIQUE
CHANNEL**

Rio Ligonha

Iuluti   Muatua   Rio Menomone

Rio Methli

Namaponda

Mamala

Nacapa

Quinga

Chalaua

Ponta Selela

▼ **37** ▼

236

15°S

270

243

40°

39°E

21 ▲

A   B   15   C   D

0   10   20 km
0   5   10 mi

▲ 26 ▲

E   F   G   H

Otjozondjupa

To Ondangwa
(66km)

Oshivelo
Von Mushara
Lindequist
Gate   Mokuti
Mokuti

19°S

Oshana
Oshavelo

Twee
Palms
Fischer's Pan   Fort
Namutoni
Dikdik Drive

Otjikoto

B1

Ombuga
Omuramba
River

Kameeldoring

Mushara

Anse
Tsumcor   Namutoni
Groot Okevi
Klein Okevi   Klein Namutoni
Chudob
Kalkheuwel

Tsam

ETOSHA
NATIONAL
PARK

Dungariespomp

Andoni
Andoni Plain

Stinkwater

Springbokfontein
Ngobib
Batia   Kawaseb
Koinseb

Eland
Drive

Leeunes

Okerfontein

C40

Goas
Naunses   158   Nomiams
Naumses   Rhino   Helio
Drive
Halali
Rietfontein

Poacher's Point

E   T   O   S   H   A   P   A   N

Etosha Lookout

Kunene

Nepele
River

kwoshigumbo   River

Salvadora
Sueda
Chudobsaub

Aus

Gonob   Olifantbad
Honob
Gonob
Peninsula

Ekuma River

NAMIBIA

Gonob

Gemsbokvlakte

Ondongab

ETOSHA
NATIONAL
PARK

Kapupuhedi

Okondeka

Wolfsnes
Leeubron   Gaseb   20
Okaukuejo
Ombika   Andersson Gate   Toshari
Inn
Ongava
Lodge   To Outjo
(80km)

Natukanaoka Pan

Adamax
Nacto

Sprokieswoud
(Haunted Forest)

Grünewald

Game Fence

Oshana

Otjivalunda Pans

Okhama Pan

To Otjovasandu
(112km)
Ozonjuitiji m'Bari

Mon Desir

National Park west of Ozonjuitiji m'Bari
is restricted to tour operators and
closed to the public

▲ 25 ▲

▼ 25 ▼

E   F   G   H

1

2

3

4

5

6

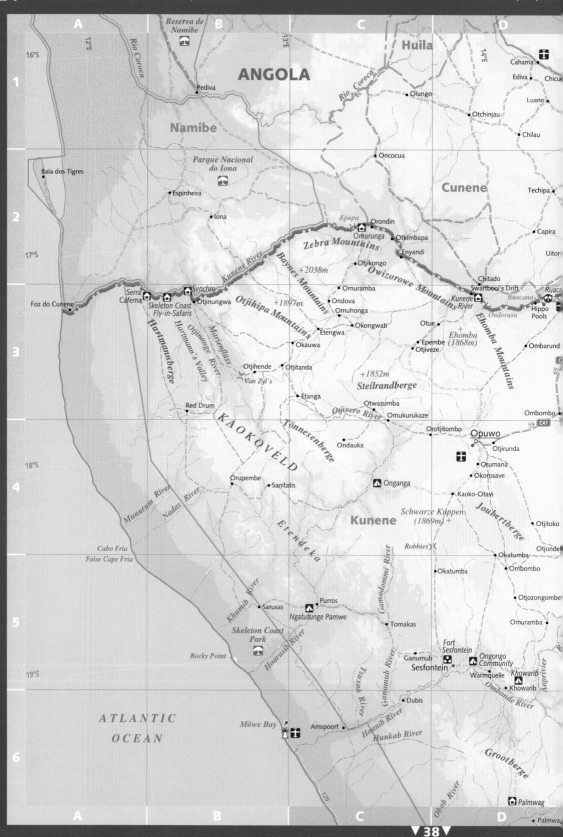

ANGOLA

Namibe

Huila

Cunene

Reserva de Namibe

Pediva

Rio Coroca

Olungo

Otchinjau

Cahama

Ediva

Chicu

Luano

Chilau

Baia dos Tigres

Parque Nacional do Iona

Espinheira

Iona

Oncocua

Techipa

Capira

Uitor

Zebra Mountains +2038m

Orondin

Omurunga

Otkimbapa

Enyandi

Chitado

Swartbooi's Drift

Ruacana

Ruacana

Foz do Cunene

Serra Cafema

Skeleton Coast Fly-in-Safaris

Synchro

Otjinungwa

Kunene River

Baynes Mountains

Otjikongo

Owizorowe Mountains

Omuramba

Ondova

Omuhonga

Okongwati

Otue

Epembe

Otjiveze

+Ehomba (1868m)

Kunene River

Ondorusu

Hippo Pools

Ombarund

Otjihipa Mountains +1897m

Etengwa

Okauwa

Otjihende

Otjitanda

Van Zyl's

Marienfluss

Otjinange River

Hartmann's Valley

Hartmannberge

Red Drum

K A O K O V E L D

Steilrandberge +1852m

Etanga

Otwazumba

Omukurukaze

Orotjitombo

Opuwo

Otjirunda

59 C41

Otjivero River

Tönnesenberge

Ondauka

Orupembe

Sanitatis

Onganga

Orumana

Okorosave

Kaoko-Otavi

Kunene

Schwarze Kuppen (1869m) +

Otjitoko

Otjonde

Joubertberge

Munutum River

Nadas River

Cabo Fria

False Cape Fria

E r e n d e k a

Robbies)(

Okatumba

Ombombo

Okatumba

Otjozongombe

Omuramba

Khumib River

Sarusas

Purros

Ngatutunge Pamwe

Tomakas

Skeleton Coast Park

Rocky Point

Hoarusib River

Gamdolomni River

Tsuxab River

Ganumub River

Ganumub

Fort Sesfontein

Sesfontein

Ongongo Community

Warmquelle

Khowarib

Khowarib

Ombonde River

Kaprivier

Dubis

A T L A N T I C

O C E A N

Möwe Bay

Amsport

Hoanib River

Hunkab River

Grootberge

Obob River

Palmwag

Palmwa

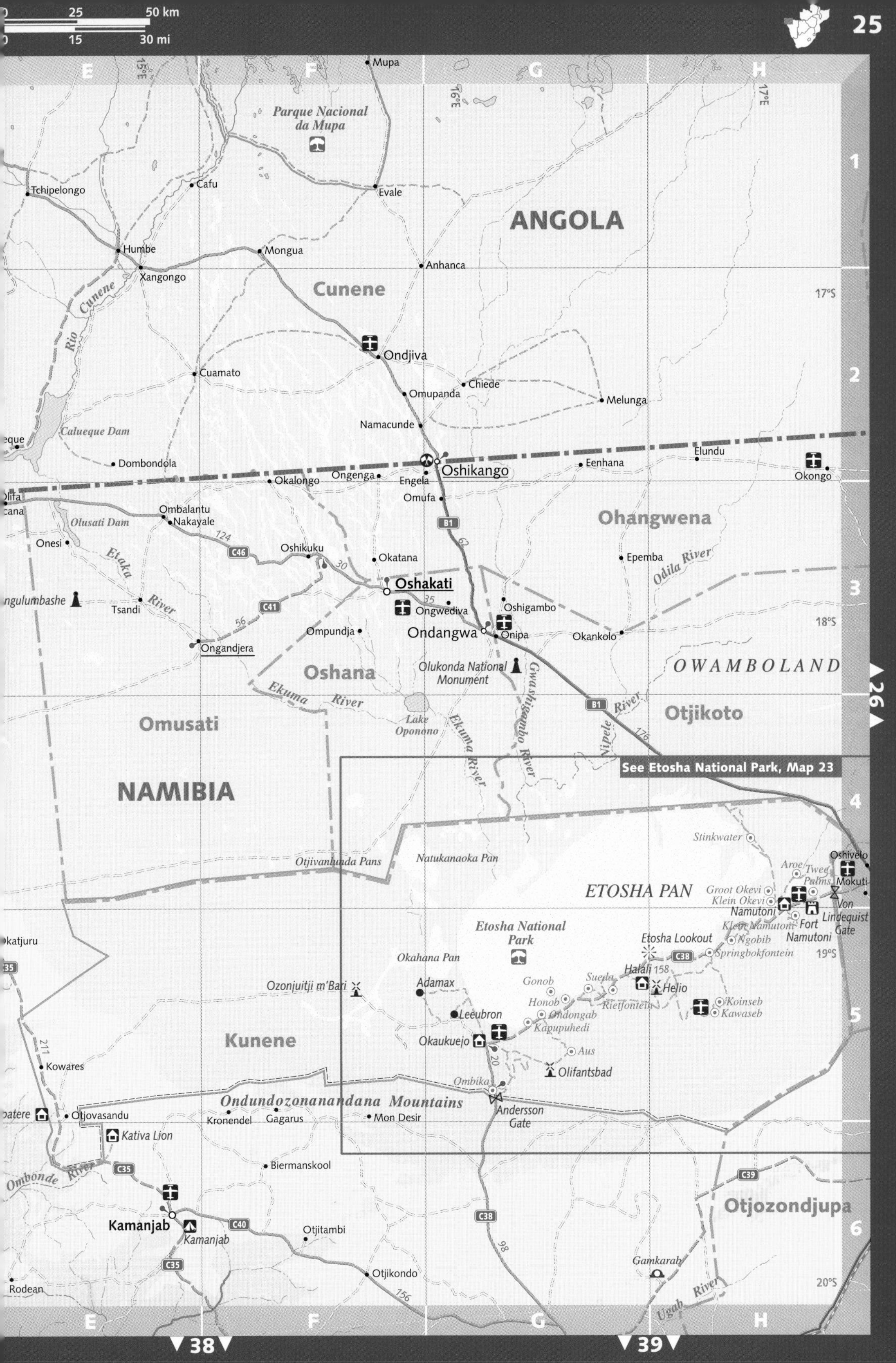

0 25 50 km
0 15 30 mi
E
F
G
H
15°E
16°E
17°E
17°S
18°S
19°S
20°S
1
2
3
4
5
6
Mupa
Parque Nacional da Mupa
Tchipelongo
Cafu
Evale
ANGOLA
Humbe
Xangongo
Mongua
Anhanca
Cunene
Rio Cunene
Ondjiva
Cuamato
Chiede
Omupanda
Melunga
Namacunde
Calueque Dam
Dombondola
Oshikango
Elundu
Eenhana
Okongo
Okalongo
Ongenga
Engela
Omufa
Ohangwena
Ombalantu
Nakayale
Olusati Dam
Onesi
C46
124
B1
62
Oshikuku
Okatana
Epemba
Odila River
Etaka River
30
Oshakati
35
Tsandi
C41
Ongwediva
Oshigambo
56
Ompundja
Ondangwa
Onipa
Okankolo
Ongandjera
Oshana
Olukonda National Monument
OWAMBOLAND
Ekuma River
Gwashigambo River
Nipele River
Otjikoto
Omusati
Lake Oponono
176
NAMIBIA
See Etosha National Park, Map 23
Stinkwater
Oshivelo
Natukanaoka Pan
Otjivanhanda Pans
Aroe
Twee Palms
Mokuti
ETOSHA PAN
Groot Okevi
Klein Okevi
Namutoni
Von Lindequist Gate
Fort Namutoni
Klein Namutoni
Ngobib
Etosha National Park
Etosha Lookout
C38
Springbokfontein
Okahana Pan
Halali 158
Helio
Ozonjuitji m'Bari
Adamax
Gonob
Sueda
Honob
Rietfontein
Koinseb
Kawaseb
Leeubron
Ondongab
Kapupuhedi
Kunene
Okaukuejo
Aus
20
Olifantsbad
Okatjuru
C35
Ombika
211
Kowares
Ondundozonanandana Mountains
Andersson Gate
Otjovasandu
Kronendel
Gagarus
Mon Desir
Kativa Lion
Biermanskool
Ombonde River
C39
Otjozondjupa
Kamanjab
C40
Otjitambi
C38
98
Gamkarab
Rodean
Otjikondo
156
Ugab River
26
38
39

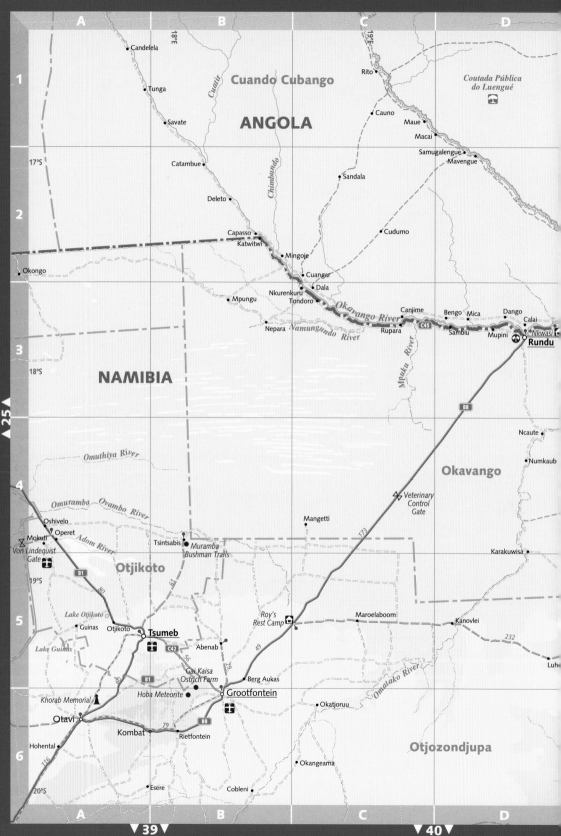

A · B · C · D

Candelela

Cuando Cubango

Rito

Coutada Pública
do Luengué

1

Tunga

Cuatir

ANGOLA

Cauno

Maue

Macai

Savate

Samugalengue

Mavengue

17°S

Catambue

Chimbando

Sandala

Deleto

2

Cudumo

Capasso

Katwitwi

Mingoje

Okongo

Cuangar

Dala

Nkurenkuru

Tondoro

Canjime

Bengo

Mica

Dango

Mpungu

Okavango River

C45

Calai

Namungundo River

Rupara

Sambiu

Mupini

Nkwasi

Nepara

Mpuku River

Rundu

3

18°S

NAMIBIA

▲25▲

B8

Ncaute

Numkaub

Omuthiya River

Okavango

4

Omuramba

Ovambo River

Mangetti

Veterinary
Control
Gate

Oshivelo

Operet

Mokuti

Adom River

Tsintsabis

Muramba
Bushman Trails

173

Karakuwisa

Von Lindequist
Gate

19°S

Otjikoto

Lake Otjikoto

80

171

Roy's
Rest Camp

Maroelaboom

Kanovlei

232

5

Guinas

Otjikoto

Tsumeb

Luhe

Lake Guinas

C42

Abenab

49

Berg Aukas

Omatako River

B1

Gai Kaisa
Ostrich Farm

56

79

Hoba Meteorite

Grootfontein

Okatjoruu

Khorab Memorial

Otavi

B8

Otjozondjupa

Hohental

Kombat

79

Rietfontein

Okangeama

6

Esere

Cobleni

20°S

A · B · C · D

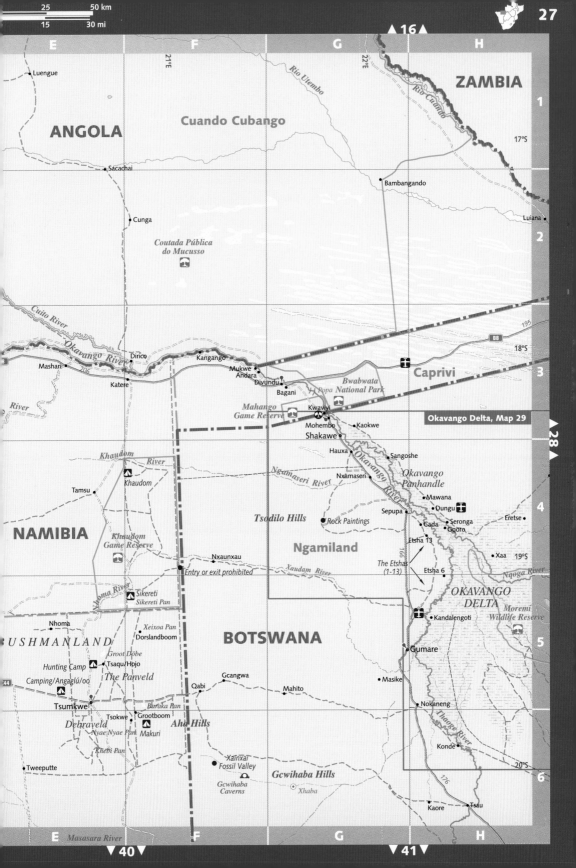

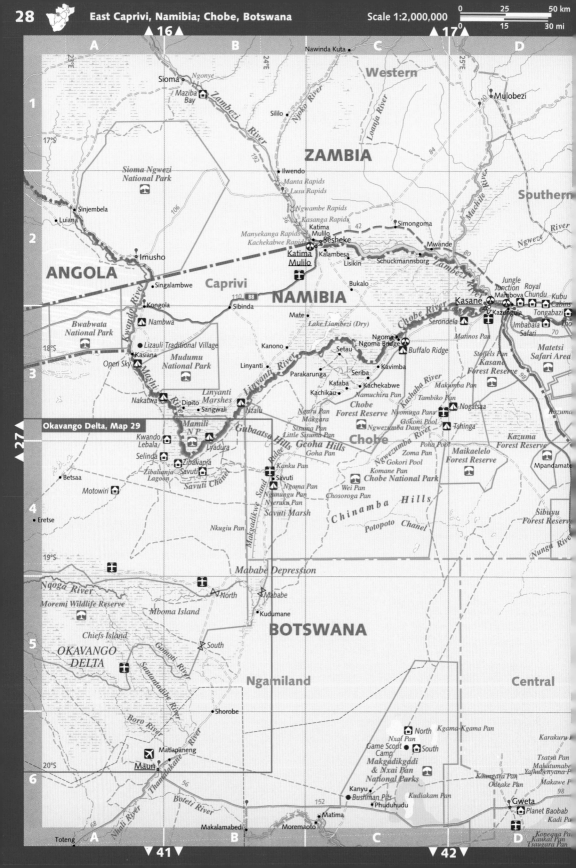

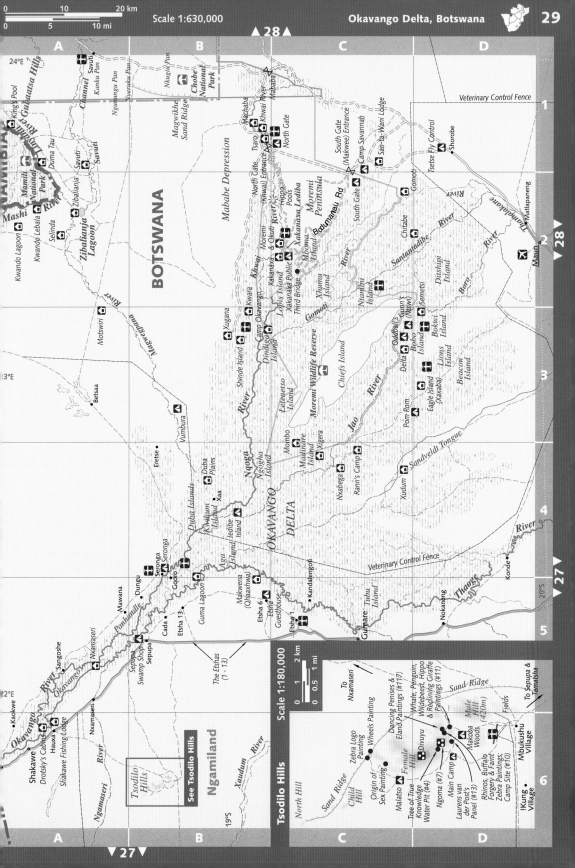

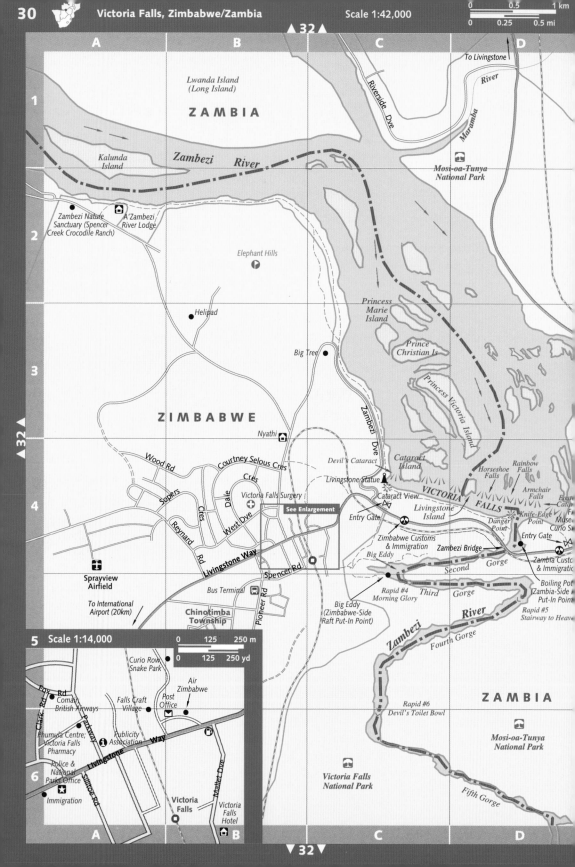

0   0.5   1 km
0   0.25   0.5 mi

32

A   B   C   D

1

Lwanda Island
(Long Island)

ZAMBIA

To Livingstone

Riverside Dve

Marumba River

32

Kalunda
Island

Zambezi River

Mosi-oa-Tunya
National Park

2

Zambezi Nature
Sanctuary (Spencer
Creek Crocodile Ranch)

A'Zambezi
River Lodge

Elephant Hills

Princess
Marie
Island

3

Helipad

Big Tree

Prince
Christian Is

Zambezi Dve

Princess Victoria Island

ZIMBABWE

32

Wood Rd

Courtney Selous Cres

Nyathi

Devil's Cataract

Cataract
Island

Horseshoe
Falls

Rainbow
Falls

Cres

Livingstone Statue

VICTORIA

Armchair
Falls

4

Sopers

Dale

Cres

Victoria Falls Surgery

See Enlargement

Cataract View

Entry Gate

Livingstone
Island

FALLS

Knife-Edge
Point

Entry Gate

Eastern
Cataract
Fal
Muse

Curio S

Reynard

West Dve

Danger
Point

Zimbabwe Customs
& Immigration

Zambezi Bridge

Rd

Livingstone Way

Big Eddy

Zambia Custo
& Immigratio

Sprayview
Airfield

Spencer Rd

Second

Gorge

Boiling Pot
(Zambia-Side
Put-In Point)

Bus Terminal

Rapid #4
Morning Glory

Third

Gorge

Rapid #5
Stairway to Heave

To International
Airport (20km)

Chinotimba
Township

Pioneer Rd

Big Eddy
(Zimbabwe-Side
Raft Put-In Point)

Zambezi

River

Fourth Gorge

Scale 1:14,000

5

0   125   250 m
0   125   250 yd

Rapid #6
Devil's Toilet Bowl

ZAMBIA

Curio Row;
Snake Park

Air
Zimbabwe

Fox Rd

Comair
British Airways

Falls Craft
Village

Post
Office

Mosi-oa-Tunya
National Park

Clark Rd

Parkway

Publicity
Association

Livingstone Way

Phumula Centre;
Victoria Falls
Pharmacy

Mallet Dve

6

Police &
National
Parks Office

Immigration

Victoria Falls
National Park

Fifth Gorge

Victoria
Falls

Victoria
Falls Hotel

Mallett Dve

A   B   C   D

32

0   50   100 m
0   50   100 yd

▲ 29 ▲

E   **F**   **G**   **H**

North-west Entrance

Sunken Passageway
Main or North Entrance

HILL COMPLEX
(NHARIRIRE YA MAMBO)

See Hill Complex

Central
Parallel Passage

Inner
Perimeter
Wall

Altar
Stone

Outer
Parallel
Passage

Enclosure 1

Ancient
Daga Hut
Remains

Stone
Pillars

Inner Parallel
Passage

West Entrance

Chevron Pattern Wall

Outer Perimeter Wall

Daga
Platform

Stepped
Platform

Green
Schist
Stones

Grooved
Buttresses

1

2

Great Zimbabwe
Hotel

Conical
Tower

Small
Tower

0   10   20 m
0   10   20 yd

Scale 1:1,500   **Great Enclosure (Imba Huru)**

Reconstructed
Karanga Village

Small
Conical
Tower

National
Emblem Bird
Found Here

3

RIDGE
ENCLOSURES

VALLEY
ENCLOSURES

▲ 34 ▲

Sunken Passageway

EASTERN RIDGE
ENCLOSURES

Stone Walls

4

THE GREAT ENCLOSURE
(IMBA HURU)

Boulders & Rocky outcrops

See Great Enclosure

0   10   20 m
0   10   20 yd

Scale 1:1,000   **Hill Complex (Nharirire Ya Mambo)**

5

Cleft Rock
Enclosure

Summit

Main Entrance

Western
Enclosure

Eastern
Enclosure

Gold
Furnace
Enclosure

Original
Covered
Entrance

Central
Passage

6

Pit

Southern
Enclosures

Recess
Enclosure

E   **F**   **G**   **H**

▼ 45 ▼

Bilili Hot Springs
Dumdumwezi
Choma
Batoka
Pemba   Gwembe
Southern   Chipepo   Forty Mile Island   Tashi
Bumi Hills
Kalomo   Tara
Lake Kariba   Mashonaland
Lake Kariba
Recreational Park   Sinamwenda   West
Bowwood   Chete
Safari Area   Chifudzi River
Sipatunyana   Siasibabole   Sinazeze
Zimba   Kachele   Sinazongwe   Mapongola Hill
Maamba   Mwera   Chete Island
Sikula Island
Kabanga   Chikauka Islands   Siabuwa   Manyabe Vlei
Matunga
ZAMBIA   Sijarira   Gonde Vlei
Forest Area
Senkobo   Mucheni
Binga   Kaswiswi   Chizarira Hills
Livingstone   Chizarira   Sipanti Vl
Victoria Falls, Map 30   National Park   Busi
Pokuma   Sebungwe River   Chirisa
Zambezi   Mlibizi   Safari Area
National   Livingstone   Kariyangwe
Park   Victoria   Mosi-oa-Tunya   Batoka Gorge   Zambezi River   Msuna   Lusulu   Mufima
Victoria Falls   National Park   Mouth   Tjibuli   Ntaba-Ma
Taita   Deka   Mlibizi River   Sekomela Pan   Sibilo Vlei   Midland
Victoria Falls   Falcon   Drum   Mzola   Zikamanus
International   Matetsi River   Deka River   Safari Area   Matobolo Flats
Banda-Masuie Forest Land   Gwaai River   Cewali Pan   Lutope Ri
Kazuma Pan   Matetsi   Thomson Junction   Kamativi   Kana River
National Park   Matetsi Headquarters   Deka   Sefula Pan
Kazuma Forest Land   Hwange   Entuba   Gwaai River   Lubimbi
Matetsi   Hwange   Dete Crossroads   ZIMBABWE
Pandamatenga   Safari Area   Bumbusi   Deka   Safari Crossroads   Sidoba Sine Danka Pan
Nantwich   Sinamatella   Chokamella   Gwaai River   Tshotsholo
Sebutu   Robins   Dete   Simba   Allan Wilson
Cauchi Pan   Umkombo   Memorial   Tshwali Pan
Tshoroko Pan   Masuma Dam   Garangwe Pan   Hwange Main   Ngamo
Sinuyu   Shumba   Dom Pan   Kennedy Pans   Forest Land   Lupane
Forest Reserve   Mandavi Dam   Valalla Pan   Nyangindhlovu Pan   Lupane River   Hlaw
Dandari Pan   Shumba Pan   Shapi Pan   Zemba Pan   Kennedy   Kenmaur   Gwampa River
Tibokai Pan (Dry)   Inyoni Pan   Jambile Pan   Munyai Pan   Ngamo   Lake Alic
Dadadda Pan   Samavumdhlu Pan   Makalawa Pans   Forest Lar
Hwange National Park   Ngwethla Pan   Ngamo Pans   Bubi River
Naconichi Pan   Magunyaan Pans   Gwaai   Gwaai
Toga Pans   Forest Land
Shechechi Pans   Chemuumi River   Mlagisa   Bembezi River
Korodziba   Gwaai   Insuza River
Nkana Pan   Matabeleland North   Sawmills
Central   Pelendaba   Ningombeneshango   Insezi   Umguza River
Tamasanka Pan   Dhlamini   Forest Land
Kauklakla Pan   Ngoma   Mabiriya   Mkubazi   Highfields
Sibaninhi Pan   Jolume   Madziba   Insezi River   Nyamandh
Karakuru Pan   Tsebanana   Tsholotsho   Khami River
BOTSWANA   Basutos   Tsuli   Tshwadini Pan   Redba
Mahutumabe Pan   Limpopa Pan   Ngwatene Pan   Mgwagwa Pan   Mbamba
Nata River   Maitengwe River   Ndolwane   Ngwita Pan   Nshaba   Khami
Mengwe   Maitengwe   Hingwe   Madhlambudzi   Chesa
Zoroga   Nata   Kgokwane   Forest Land
Tsigara   Nata Delta   Nkange   Matabeleland South   Khami

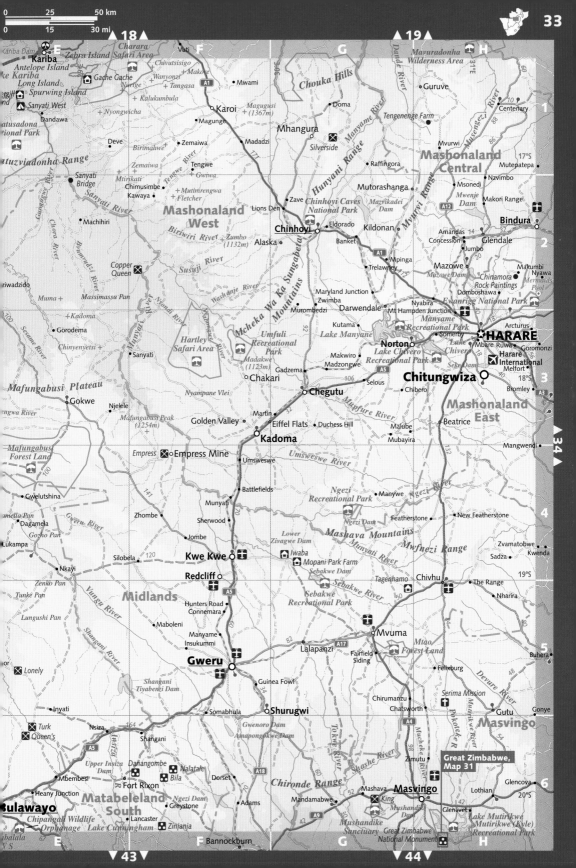

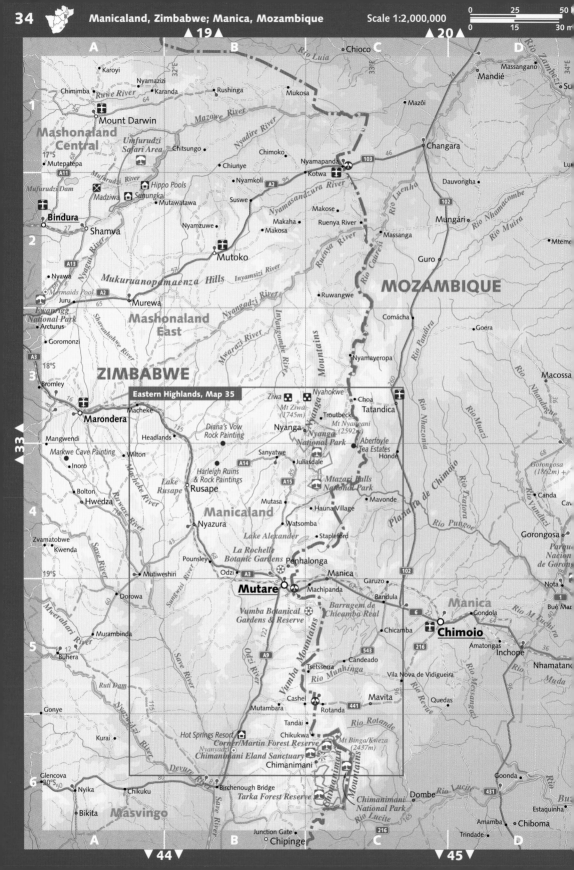

Map showing Manicaland, Zimbabwe and Manica, Mozambique region.

Scale markings: 0 25 50 (km); 15 30 m

Grid references: A B C D across top and bottom; 1–6 down sides.

Places and features:

Karoyi, Chimimba, Nyamazizi, Karanda, Ruwe River, Rushinga, Mukosa, Chioco, Rio Luia, Massangano, Mandié, Rio Zambezi, Su—

Mount Darwin, Mashonaland Central, Umfurudzi Safari Area, Chitsungo, Chiunye, Nyamkoli, Chimoko, Nyamapanda, Kotwa, Mazôi, Changara, Dauvonhga, A11, Mutepetepa

Mufurudzi River, Hippo Pools, Madziwa, Sunungkai, Mutawatawa, Suswe, A2, Nyamasanaxura River, Makose, Massanga, Mungári, Rio Muira, Mtemé

Bindura, Shamva, Nyamzuwe, Makaha, Makosa, Makose, Ruenya River, Rio Luenha, Rio Nhamacombe, 102

A13, Nyawa, Nyagui River, Mukuruanopamaenza Hills, Inyamsizi River, Murewa, Ruwangwe, Rio Cauresi, Guro, MOZAMBIQUE

Mermaids Pool, Juru, A2, Nyangadzi River, Inyangombe River, Ruenya River, Comácha, Goera, Rio Pandira

Ewanrigg National Park, Arcturus, Goromonzi, Shavanhohwe River, Mwarazi River, Nyanga Mountains, Nyamayeropa, Rio Nhazonia, Macossa, Rio Nhamacomba

A3, Bromley, 18°S, ZIMBABWE, Mashonaland East, Eastern Highlands, Map 35, Ziwa, Mt Ziwa (1745m), Nyahokwe, Choa, Tatandica, Rio Nhazonia

Marondera, Macheke, Diana's Vow Rock Painting, Nyanga, Nyanga National Park, Mt Nyangani (2592m), Aberfoyle Tea Estates, Honde, Gorongosa (1862m), Canda, Cav—

Mangwendi, Headlands, Wilton, Sanyatwe, Juliasdale, A14, A15, Mtazari Halls National Park, Mavonde

Markwe Cave Painting, Inoro, Harleigh Ruins & Rock Paintings, Rusape, Lake Rusape, Mutasa, Hauna Village, Rio Chimaio, Rio Txiora, Canda

Bolton, Hwedza, Ruware River, Macheke River, Nyazura, Manicaland, Lake Alexander, Watsomba, Stapleford, Planalto de Chimaio, Rio Pungoe, Gorongosa

Zvamatobwe, Kwenda, Save River, Sungwezi River, Pounsley, La Rochelle Botanic Gardens, Penhalonga, Manica, Garuzo, 102, Parque Nacion de Gorong—, Nota

19°S, Mutiweshiri, Odzi, A3, Mutare, Machipanda, Bandula, Manica, Bué Mar—, Rio M Luchira

Dorowa, Odzi River, Vumba Botanical Gardens & Reserve, Barragem de Chieamba Real, Chicamba, Chimoio, Gondola, 6, 216, Amatongas

Murambinda, A9, Vumba Mountains, 543, Candeado, Inchope, Rio Messangaci, Rio Muda, Nhamatand—

Buhera, 12, Ruti Dam, Tsetssera, Rio Munhinga, Vila Nova de Vidigueira, Rio Revue, Quedas

Gonye, Nyanyadzi River, Mutambara, Cashel, Rotanda, 441, Mavita, Rio Rotande

Glencova, 20°S, 60, Hot Springs Resort, Corner/Martin Forest Reserve, Chikukwa, Tandai, Mt Binga/Kweza (2437m), Chimanimani Mountains

Nyika, Chikuku, Devure River, Birchenough Bridge, Chimanimani Eland Sanctuary, Chimanimani, Rio Rotande, Dombe, Rio Lucite, 431, Goonda

Bikita, Masvingo, Tarka Forest Reserve, Save River, Chimanimani National Park, Rio Lucite, Estaquinha, Bui—

Junction Gate, Chipinge, 216, Amamba, Chiboma, Trindade

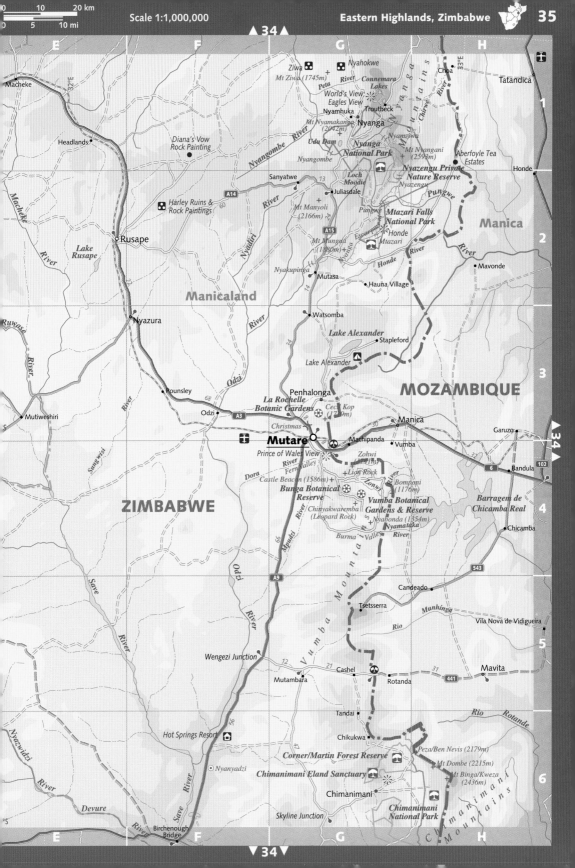

▲20▲   ▲21▲

A   **B**   **C**   **D**

Maravenge Range

MALAWI

Nchalo
Sucoma Sugar Factory
N'gabu   Elephant Marsh
Sorgin
Bangula
Dande
Mchacha James
Makhanga
Chiromo
Chire
Mwabvi
Wildlife Reserve
Mwabvi Wildlife Reserve

Zoa
Rio Liase
Gema
Môngué
Monte Chiperone
(2054m)
Licíro
Metolola

Chá Lugela
Limbuè
Chá Madal
Monte Mabu
(1710m)
Tacuane
Vulalo

229

Lugela

1

Bandar
Tambara
Ancuaze
Doa
Chiramba
Lundo
17°S

Rio Minjova
Rio

Chembo
Nsanje
Lulwe   Marka
Vila Nova da Fronteira

Morire
Chametengo
Megaza
Muandiua

Macatanja
Maticula
Muávula
Marraca
Chitu
Derre

149
Rio Luala
Rio Lugela

2

Madzuire   Sança
Molima
Rio Pompue
Rio

Chemba
Vila de Sena   Nhamalabué
Mutarara
Goma
Charre
Pinda
Sabe
Chipanga

Monte Morrumbala
(1172m)

Morrumbala
Rio Meruatonjie
Rio Luala
Rio Munguze
Rio Licuara

Sanandere
213
34

3

Canxixe
Gombalançai
Maringué
Sando
18°S
Rio Nhamacurra
128
EN1
Nhamacolomo

Rio Mepuse
Chindio
Caia
Matondo
32
58
108
Rio Zangue

Mopeia
Missão Conho
Lacerdónia
Chupanga
219

Zambézia
Nicoadala
Campo
225
100
56
Rio Cuacua

Quelimane

Rio Longosa
Rio Mutade
Rio Zambeze
Muto River
Negoa
Mucupia
Abreu

▲34▲

4

Piro
215
Inhaminga
Mazamba
442
126
Condué

Parque Nacional
de Gorongosa

Inhamitanga
112
213

M o z a m b i q u e
P l a n í c i e   D e   Rio Salone
Patalás
Rio Nhapacue

Marromeu
Luabo
Micaúne
Chinde
Conceição
Muiembe

Rio Muzelo
Rio Murgari
Rio Malingapansi

Ponta Timbue

MOZAMBIQUE

5

Chitengo
443
Muanza
Bué Maria
70
Sofala
Rio Pungoe
Semacueza
213
Nessona
Rio Sanga
Reserva de
Marromeu

Chiniziua
Machesse

Nhamatanda
Lamege
Muda   Tica
Macuácua
Rio Sanguassi
Rio Sambezo

EN6
214
Dondo
Savane

6

Nova Almada   Búzi
Bandua
Manica
Rio Búzi
20°S

Beira International
Beira

▼45▼

A   **B**   **C**   **D**

0 25 50 km
0 15 30 mi

E **F** **G** **H**

Nipiodi
Mucúbi
Nampevo
Rio Licungo
Rio Meleta
Uape
Mamala
Nacapa
Chalaua
16°S
Rio Metuli
Missão
Intúrro
Gilé
Nampula
Mária
Mulevala
Morrua
38°E
Etaga
Rio Larde
Metil
Jeque
Aúbe
104
Rio Nipiode
Reserva do Gilé
Rio Molocue
Metana
Larde
260
Maneia
Rio Malema
Rio Ligonha
See Inset
1
Mocuba
Rio Meleta
Regone
Nova Nabúri
Moma
Mucubela
Mualama
Ilha de Moma
2
Rio Raraga
485
Rio Monga
Notocote
Ponta Lipobane
Ponta Macalonga
Cariua
230
Bajone
Moebase
17°S
Rio Licungo
226
Olinga
Pebane
Ilha de Casuarina
Nante
Murroa
Ponta Monaepa
Ilha de Fogo
3
Namacurra
Palva
Mualoa
Macuze
Carrafa
Sopinho
Zalala
Mundimo (Madal)

18°S

4

M O Z A M B I Q U E   C H A N N E L

5

19°S

Ponta Selela
16°S
236
Boila
40°E
Angoche
Aúbe
Quilúa
Ilha de Mafamede
Larde
6

E **F** **G** **H**

▲ 24 ▲   ▲ 25 ▲

A   B   C   D

Rodean

Palmwag
Palmwag

Grootberge

Obob River

129
13°E

Terrace Bay
Terrace Bay

Uniab River

1
20°S

Torra Bay
Torra Bay
Palgrave Point

C34

Koichab River

Springbokwater

Bergsig

C39

Huab River

Kunene

Petrified Forest

212

Tutara

15°E
105

Huab River

Fransfontein

Franfonteinberge

Aba-Huab River

Khorixas

C39

Gainatseb

Vingerklip
Vingerklip

Omt

Epur

DAMARALAND

Skeleton Coast Park

Toscanini

Skeleton Coast

NAMIB

2

Twyfelfontein
Rock Engravings

Aba-Huab

Wondergat
Organ Pipes

+ Brandtberg

Doros Crater

Sorris Sorris

Ozondati

Omangambo

Omatjet

+ Okonyenya
(1902m)

Ugab River

C35

117

3
21°S

Ogden Rocks

Durissa Bay

Bandom Bay
Myl 108
Bocock's Bay

Ugabmund Park Office

Goboboseberge

Messum Crater

Brandberg West

The Brandberg

Königstein
(2573m) +

Tsisab Ravine

Numas Ravine

Uis

Okombache

Neineis

Uigaran

ATLANTIC

OCEAN

DESERT

178

C34

Horing Bay
Cape Cross Bay
Cape Cross

Cape Cross Seal Reserve

National West Coast
Recreation Area

Myl 72

46

C35

102

Onamura River

Erongoberge

Spitzkoppe
(1728m) +

+ Klein Spitzkoppe
(1584m)

1

4
22°S

Henties Bay

Jakkalsputz

Erongo

81

Ebony

Trekkopje
Monument
Trekkopje

Khan R

Arandis

Otjipateraber

5

Wlotzkas Baken

Rock Bay
Myl 14

Swakopmund

B2

C34

Rössing
Rössing

Khan

Welwitschia
Plains

C28

Groot T

Bloedkoppi

Namib Desert Park

6

Pelican Point

Walvis
Bay

Walvis Bay

Rooikop

Vogelfederberg

C14

+ Vogelfederberg

Hamiltonberge
(649m)

Rooibank

Klipneus

Hamilton Hills

Mir
(8

Kaiseb

Sandwich Harbour
Marine Reserve

Sandwich Harbour
Lagoon

Anichab

Sandwich Harbour

Gobabed Desert
Ecological Research Unit

Gor

River

Hor

Mirabib

Tropic of Capricorn

23°S

A   B   C   D

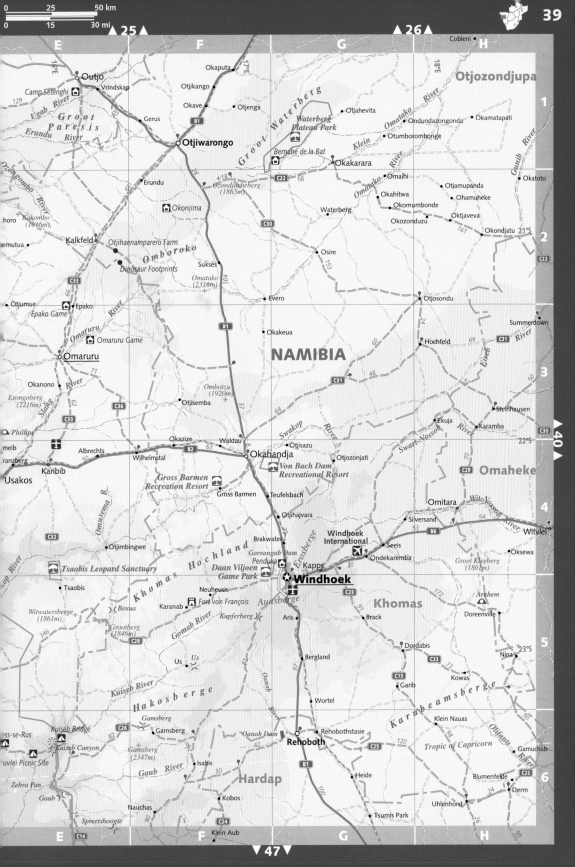

0   25   50 km
0   15   30 mi

Otjozondjupa

Cobleni

E   F   G   H

1

Camp Setenghi
Outjo
Vrindskap
Ugab River
129
Groot
Paresis
River
Erundu
Okaputa
Otjikango
Okave
Otjenga
Gerus
B1
Otjiwarongo
Groot Waterberg
Waterberg
Plateau Park
Bernabé de la Bat
Otjahevita
Ondundazongonda
Omatako River
Okamatapati
Klein
Otumborombonge
C22
58
Omaihi
Okatoto
Okahitwa
Otjamupanda
Ohamuheke
Omatako
Okomumbonde
Oktjaveva
Okozonduzu
Okondjatu 21°S
167

2

Kokombo
(1616m)
Kalkfeld
C33
Otjihaenamparero Farm
Dinosaur Footprints
Omboroko
Sukses
+18
Ozondjacheberg
(1865m)
Okonjima
Waterberg
Omatako
(2316m)
Osire
Otjosondu
Summerdown
C31
C22

3

Otjimue
Epako
Epako Game
Omaruru Game
Omaruru
71
Okanono
Erongoberg
(2216m)
Slang
River
C33
C36
Otjisemba
Ombotzu
(1920m)
Okakeua
Evero
NAMIBIA
C31
48
Hochfeld
69
Ekuja
Karamba
Steinhausen
Eiseb River
60
24
Swakop River
C30
40
22°S

4

Phillips
meib
ranzberg
Karibib
Usakos
Albrechts
Wilhelmstal
Okazize
B2
Waldau
Okahandja
Otjisazu
Otjozonjati
Swart-Nossob River
70
C29
Omaheke
Omitara
Wit-Nossob River
54
Witvlei
Oksewa
Groot Kleeberg
(1801m)
Gross Barmen
Recreation Resort
Gross Barmen
Teufelsbach
Von Bach Dam
Recreational Resort
Otjihajvara
Silversand
53
B6

5

C32
Otjimbingwe
Tsaobis Leopard Sanctuary
Tsaobis
Witwatersberge
(1861m)
346
Bosua
Grootberg
(1846m)
C28
Us
Us
Karanab
Fort von François
Neuheusis
Brakwater
Goreangab Dam
Penduka
Daan Viljoen
Game Park
Kupferberg
Gomab River
Aris
Windhoek
International
Kapps
Seeis
Ondekaremba
20
Auasberge
Brack
Khomas
172
Arnhem
Doreenville
91
Dordabis
C23
Nina
23°S

6

ess-se-Rus
Kuiseb Bridge
C26
Kuiseb Canyon
uvlei Picnic Site
Zebra Pan
Gaub
Gamsberg
Gamsberg
Gamsberg
(2347m)
Gaub River
Isabis
Nauchas
Kobos
Spreetshoogte
C14
Klein Aub
C24
Kuiseb River
Hakosberge
Us
Oanob
River
Bergland
Wortel
Oanob Dam
42
Rehobothstasie
Rehoboth
C25
120
Heide
B1
100
Tsumis Park
Hardap
Karubeamsberge
Klein Nauas
Kowas
Garib
C15
73
Tropic of Capricorn
98
Blumenfelde
Gamuchab
Olifants River
C23
24
Derm
Uhlenhorst
26
35

E   C14   F   Klein Aub   G   H

Otjozondjupa

Omaheke

Otjosondjou River

Eiseb River

19°E

20°E

21°E

Gunib River

Okatoto

21°S

Eiseb River

Rooiboklaagte River

Otjinoko River

NAMIBIA

Epukiro River

C22

Otjinene

Okanuwa

C29
Dis Al

44

Alexeck River

Summerdown

Omawewozonyanda

Epukiro River

166

Okavarumendu

Epukiro

Labora

Rietfontein River

Helena

Kanana Safari

Talismanis

Rietfontein

C30

22°S

Swart-Nossob River

118

Drimiopsis

C22

Karakubis

A2

162

Tshootsha

Otjimukandi

Xanagas

Auheib

118

Mamuno
Buitepos

Charles Hill

Margaretental

51

Witvlei

Gobabis

Makunda

Okwa River

40

Babi-Babi

Wit-Nossob River

Poortjie

Gottberg

C22

K A L A H A R I   D E S E R T

Ruimte

Keitsas

C20

Dismyne

Kule

23°S

Onderombapa

Wyoming

90

Ncojane

Gross Ums

Ukwi

Ukwi Pan

Tropic of Capricorn

C23

30

36

Leonardville

190

Nossob River

40

Aminuis

Oliffants River

Masethleng Pan

▲ 39 ▲

24°S

C20

Hoop

C22

Oorwinning

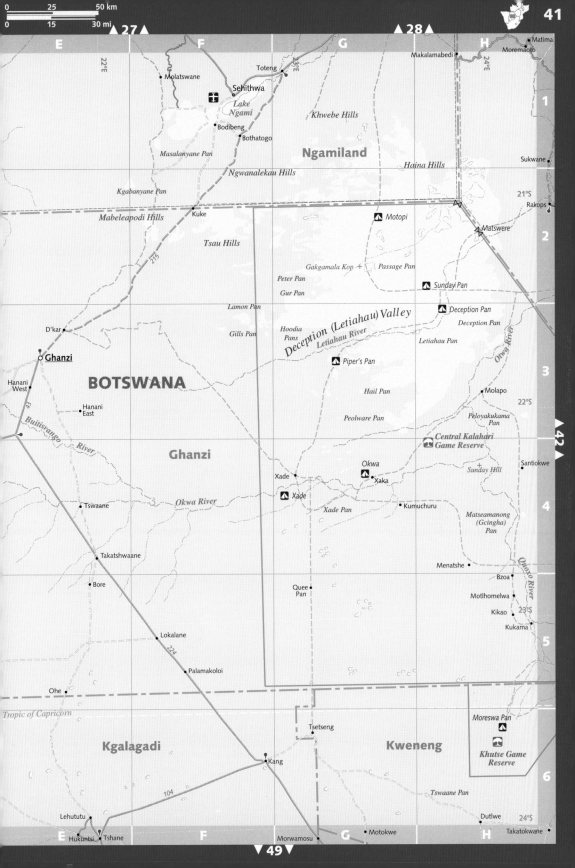

Map of Botswana (page 41)

BOTSWANA

Ngamiland

Ghanzi

Kgalagadi

Kweneng

Scale: 0 — 25 — 50 km / 0 — 15 — 30 mi

Places and features:
- Matima
- Moremaoto
- Makalamabedi
- Molatswane
- Toteng
- Sehithwa
- Lake Ngami
- Khwebe Hills
- Bodibeng
- Bothatogo
- Masalanyane Pan
- Sukwane
- Kgabanyane Pan
- Ngwanalekau Hills
- Haina Hills
- Rakops
- Mabeleapodi Hills
- Kuke
- Motopi
- Matswere
- Tsau Hills
- Gakgamala Kop
- Passage Pan
- Peter Pan
- Sunday Pan
- Gur Pan
- Lamon Pan
- Deception (Letiahau) Valley
- Deception Pan
- Hoodia Pans
- Letiahau River
- Letiahau Pan
- Otwg River
- D'kar
- Gills Pan
- Piper's Pan
- Ghanzi
- Hail Pan
- Molapo
- Hanani West
- Peolware Pan
- Peloyakukama Pan
- Hanani East
- Buitisvango River
- Central Kalahari Game Reserve
- Ghanzi
- Santiokwe
- Okwa
- Sunday Hill
- Xade
- Xaka
- Tswaane
- Okwa River
- Xade
- Xade Pan
- Kumuchuru
- Matseamanong (Gcingha) Pan
- Takatshwaane
- Menatshe
- Bzoa
- Bore
- Motlhomelwa
- Quee Pan
- Kikao
- Kukama
- Lokalane
- Okoxo River
- Palamakoloi
- Ohe
- Tropic of Capricorn
- Moreswa Pan
- Tsetseng
- Khutse Game Reserve
- Kang
- Tswaane Pan
- Lehututu
- Dutlwe
- Hukuntsi
- Tshane
- Morwamosu
- Motokwe
- Takatokwane

Grid references: E F G H, columns 1–6

Coordinates: 22°E, 23°E, 24°E, 21°S, 22°S, 23°S, 24°S

Road numbers: 275, 224, 104

Grid arrows: 27, 28, 42, 49

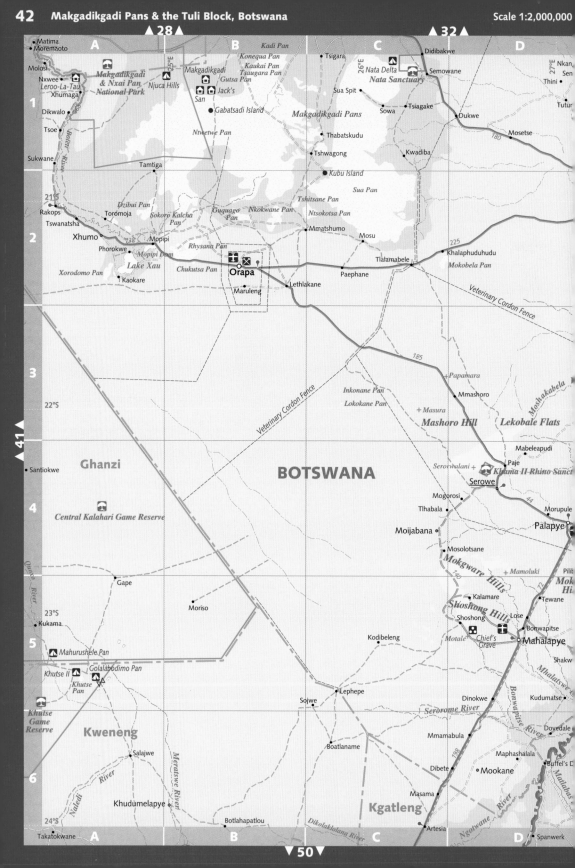

▲ 28 ▲   ▲ 32 ▲

Matima
Moremaoto
Molosi
Nxwee
Leroo-La-Tau
Xhumaga
Dikwalo
Tsoe

Makgadikgadi & Nxai Pan National Park
Njuca Hills
Makgadikgadi
Gutsa Pan
Jack's
San
Gabatsadi Island
Ntwetwe Pan

Kadi Pan
Konequa Pan
Kaukai Pan
Tsaugara Pan

Tsigara
Nata Delta
Nata Sanctuary
Sua Spit
Sowa
Tsiagake
Didibakwe
Semowane

Makgadikgadi Pans

Thabatskudu
Tshwagong
Kwadiba
Dukwe
Mosetse

Nkan
Sen
Thini
Tutur

Sukwane
Tamtiga
Kubu Island
Sua Pan

21°S
Rakops
Tswanatsha
Xhumo
Phorokwe
Mopipi
Mopipi Dam

Dzibui Pan
Toromoja
Sokoro Kalcha Pan
Guguago Pan
Nkokwane Pan
Tshitsane Pan
Ntsokotsa Pan

Mmatshumo
Mosu
Paephane
Khalaphuduhudu
Tlalamabele
Mokobela Pan

225

Xorodomo Pan
Lake Xau
Kaokare
Rhysana Pan
Chukutsa Pan
Orapa
Maruleng
Lethlakane

Veterinary Cordon Fence

185
Papamara
Inkonane Pan
Lokokane Pan
Masura
Mashoro Hill
Mmashoro
Lekobale Flats
Moshakabela

22°S

Veterinary Cordon Fence

Santiokwe

Ghanzi

BOTSWANA

Serorwalani
Khama II Rhino Sanct
Serowe
Mabeleapudi
Paje

41

Central Kalahari Game Reserve

Mogorosi
Tlhabala
Moijabana
Mosolotsane
Morupule
Palapye

44

Okwa River

Gape
Moriso
Kukama
23°S

Mokgware Hills
Mamoluki
Shoshong Hills
Kalamare
Shoshong
Lose
Tewane
Bonwapitse
Mahalapye
Shakw

Pilit
Mok
Hi

740
720

Mahurushele Pan
Khutse II
Golalabodimo Pan
Khutse Pan

Kodibeleng
Motale
Chief's Grave

Khutse Game Reserve

Kweneng

Salajwe

Meratswe River
Naledi River

Lephepe
Sojwe

Boatlaname

Dinokwe
Serorome River
Mmamabula

Kudumatse
Dovedale
Bonwapitse River

198

Khudumelapye
Botlhapatlou
Dikolaklofana River

Kgatleng

Masama
Dibete
Artesia

Mookane
Maphashalala
Buffel's D
Spanwerk

Ngotwane River
Matlabas
Mhalatswe River

Takatokwane

▼ 50 ▼

26°E   27°E

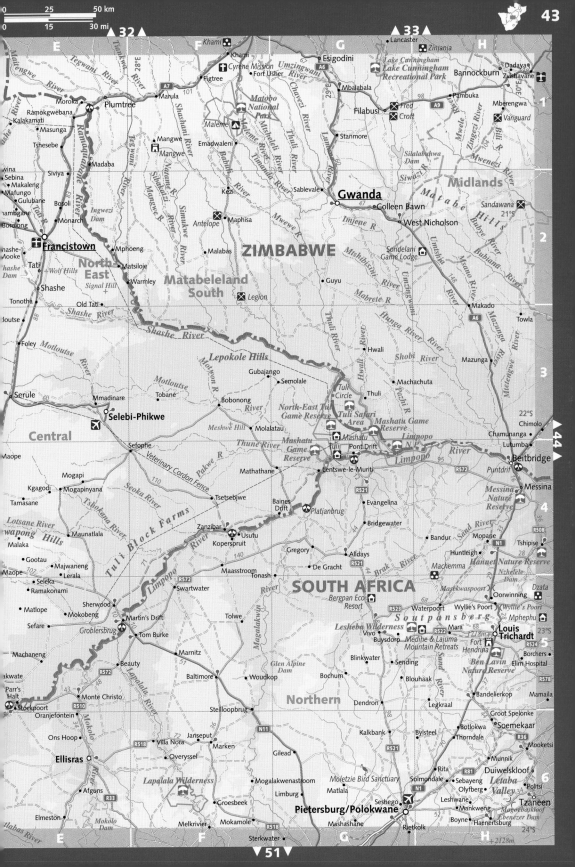

Great Zimbabwe, Map 31

Kruger NP, Map 54-55

Countries/regions: Midlands, ZIMBABWE, Masvingo, Matabeleland South, Manicaland, SOUTH AFRICA, Northern, Gaza, KRUGER NATIONAL PARK

Selected places: Zvishavane, Chivi, Mukwakwe, Ngezi, Buchwa, Sarahuru, Ngundu, Mataga, Rutenga, Mwenezi, Mbizi, Towla, Alko, Bubi, Chimolo, Chamunanga, Lutumba, Nulli, Diti, Messina, Tshipise, Dzata, Mutale, Sibasa, Thohoyandou, Ratombo, Borchers, Elim Hospital, Ha-Magoro, Mamaila, Duiwelskloof, Tzaneen, Ga-Modjadji, La Cotte, Nkambak, Letsitele, Gravelotte, Leydadorp, Phalaborwa, Namakgale, Lulekani, Murchison, Mulati, Nkomo, Giyani, Mavamba, Tshakhuma, Chredzi, Triangle, Buffalo Range, Hippo Valley, Chikombedzi, Boli, Twiza, Malapati, Sango, Chicualacuala, Chivilila, Fishan's, Sungue, Mavuè, Chitanga, Chigama, Machail, Chefu, Domasse, Muzamane, São Jorge do Limpopo, Mapai, Mepuze, Combomune, Massingir, Mabalane, Chipinge, Espungabera, Hacufera, Massangena

Rivers: Save River, Runde River, Limpopo River, Rio Save, Rio Messuize, Letaba River, Olifants

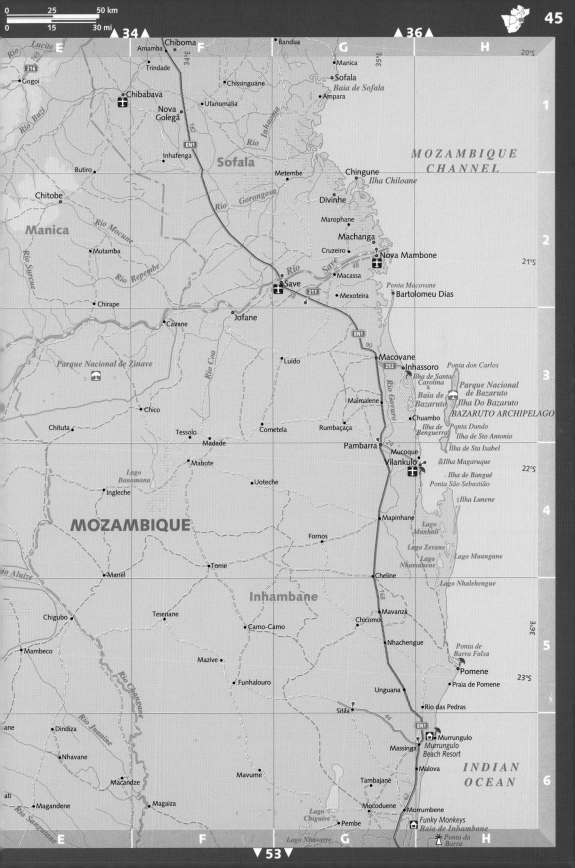

0 25 50 km
0 15 30 mi

E F G H

Rio Lucite
216
Gogoi

Chiboma
Amamba
Trindade
Chibabava
Nova Golegã

Bandua
Manica
Sofala
Baía de Sofala
Ampara

MOZAMBIQUE
CHANNEL

20°S

1

Rio Buzi
Chissinguane
Ufanomalia
Inhafenga
EN1
162

Sofala

Metembe

Chingune
Ilha Chiloane

Butiro

Rio Mocune

Divinhe

Chitobe

Rio Gorongosa

Marophane

Manica

Rio

Machanga
Cruzeiro

Ilha de Sofala

2

Mutamba

Rio Repembe

Rio Save

Save
48
Nova Mambone

21°S

Rio Surcue

Rio

Save
211
28

Macassa
Mexoteira

Ponta Macovane
Bartolomeu Dias

Chirape

Cavane
Jofane

Rio Cua

Luido

EN1
90

Macovane
Inhassoro
252

Ponta don Carlos
Ilha de Santa Carolina

3

Parque Nacional de Zinave

Chico

Rio Govuro

Malmalene

Baía de Bazaruto

Parque Nacional de Bazaruto
Ilha Do Bazaruto
BAZARUTO ARCHIPELAGO

Chituta

Tessolo
Madade

Cometela

Rumbaçaça

Chuambo

Ilha de Benguerra

Ponta Dundo
Ilha de Sto Antonio

Mabote

Pambarra

Ilha de Sta Isabel

Lago Banamana
Ingleche

Uoteche

Vilankulo
Mucoque

Ilha Magaruque
Ilha de Bangué
Ponta São Sebastião

22°S

4

MOZAMBIQUE

Fornos

Mapinhane

Ilha Lunene

Lago Manhali

Lago Zevane
Lago Nhamanene
Lago Muangane

Rio Aluize
Manel
Tome

Cheline
168

Lago Nhalehengue

Inhambane

36°E

5

Chigubo
Tesenane

Camo-Camo

Chicomo

Mavanza

Nhachengue

Ponta de Barra Falsa

Mambeco

Mazive

Funhalouro

Unguana

Pomene
Praia de Pomene

23°S

Rio Changane

Sitila

Rio das Pedras

Rio Juanine

Dindiza
Nhavane

Massinga

EN1
44

Murrungulo
Murrungulo Beach Resort

INDIAN
OCEAN

6

Macandze

Mavume

Tambajane

Malova

Rio Sangutane
Magandene

Magaiza

Mocoduene

Lago Chiguive
Pembe

Morrumbene

Funky Monkeys
Baía de Inhambane
Ponta da Barra

Lago Nhavarre

E F G H

▲ 38 ▲

	A	B	C	D

Kuiseb River

Erongo

13°E

14°E

15°E

Topnaar
Community
Hom

1

Black Cliff

Namib Desert Park

Conception Bay

NAMIBIA

24°S

Shifting Sand Dunes

2

N
A
M
I
B

Meob Bay

D
E
S
E
R
T

Black Reef

Hardap

Hollandsbird
Island ○

Black Rock

St Francis Bay

3 25°S

+Silvia Hill

+East Hill

Easter Point
Oyster Cliffs
Black Cliffs

Knoll Point

ATLANTIC OCEAN

North Point

Spencer Bay
Dolphin Head

4

+Clara H

Sadd
Hill

Hottentot Bay
Hottentot Point

26°S

Douglas Bay

Ichaboe
Island ○

Marshall Rocks ○

5

Dumfudgeon Rock

Lüderitz
Diaz Poin

Halifax Island ○
Grosse Buc

Elizabeth

6

27°S

	A	B	C	D

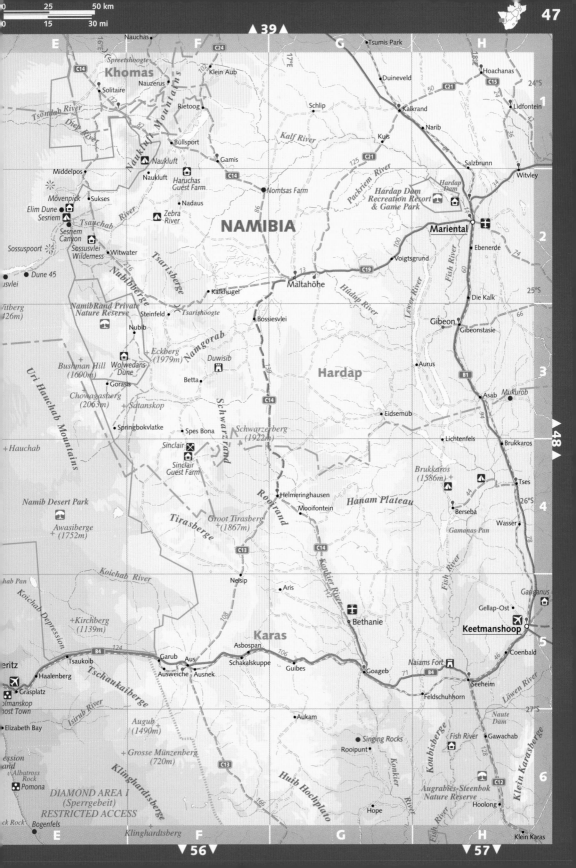

▲ 40 ▲

Grid columns: A B C D
Grid rows: 1 2 3 4 5 6

C20

24°S

Hoop

Oorwinning

Bosduin

Aranos

Vogelweide

Eirup

Stampriet

Witvley

Nossob River

Goricia

Naomi

Xchoi Pan

Dimpho Pan

Gross Nabas Farm

NAMIBIA

105

Akanous

Lendepas
Union's End

Entry or exit prohibited

Grootkolk

Swart Pan

Kgalagadi Transfrontier P

Auob River

Gochas

C18

25°S

40

Witbooisvlei

Olifants River

Omaheke

Polentswe

Langklass

Nossob River

Kwang
Lekkerwater

Sewe Panne

Nossob

Bulwana

Persip

C15

Eindpaal

Twee Rivier

C15

91

Marie Se Draai

Kgalagadi Transfrontier Park

Bitterpan

Cheleka

Dikbaardskolk

Vloorskop
+ (959m)

108

69

Welverdiend

Entry or exit prohibited
Mata Mata

Moravet

Eland

Kameelsleep

Craig Lockhart

Vaalpan

Jan

Katzies

C17

Koes

C11

Dalkeith

Auob River

Urikaruus

Kamqua

Shirley

26°S

55

Kamua

Wasser

Pulai

Montrose

C17

Garinais

109

Kubis North

138

Springboktrek Suid

Gaibis

Gemsbok Plain

Kielie
Krankie

Auchterlonie

Tier
Kop

Rooiputs

Rooiputs

Fly's Kop

Ganganus

Kokerboom Forest &
Giants Playground

C16

168

Gross Aub

Blumtal

C11

Houmoed

Samevloeiing

Twee Rivieren

Game Scout

Keetmanshoop

R360

River

Löwen

Rietfontein

Hakskeenpan

Gemshole

Bokspits

Andriesvale

Witdraai

27°S

Nordeck

Narubis

Klein Karasberge

Schroffenstein
+(2202m)

Warmfontein

Vredeshoop

55

Hardap

Uitsakpan

R31

Askham

Staansaam

107

Abiekwasputs

Koopan-Suid

Hohlweg

Obobogorap

Groot Karasberge

B1

84

Tsaraxaibis

C11

420

Davignab Suid

Gansvlei South

Noenieput

R360

170

Klein Karas

▲ 47 ▲

▲ 42 ▲

▲ 49 ▲

▼ 59 ▼

BOTSWANA

SOUTH AFRICA

Kweneng

Kgatleng

Southern

South East

North-West

Takatokwane
Mboane
Masope
Ditshegwane
Mmankgodi
Molepolole
Botlahapatlou
Letlhakeng
Lowe Rock Carvings
Dikolakiolana River
Ngotwane River
Spanwerk
Artesia
Rooibokkraal
Oliphants Drift
Lentsweletau
Sekhukhwane River
Mahetlwe
Ancient Iron Mine
Livingstone's
LMS Mission
Malotwana
Matsieng Rock Carvings
Rasesa
Bokaa
Mochudi
Pilane
Kopong
Odi
Mogoditshane
Sikwane
Malolwane
Gaborone
Tlokweng
Derdepoort
Oostermoe
Dwaalboom
Gabane
Kopfontein
Kayaseput
Thamaga
Mankgodi
Mokolodi Nature Reserve
Gaborone Dam
Ganskuil
Middelwit
Mosopa
Manyana
Mogonye
Madikwe Game Reserve
Manyana Rock Paintings
Ramotswa
Swartkopfontein
Zwingli
Wiitfonteinrand
Dwarsberg
Maokane
Ranaka
Ntlhantlhe
Otse
Nietverdiend
Silkaatskop
Mabeskraal
Pilanesberg National
Moshaneng
Kanye
Kanye
Lotlhakane
Mosenekatse Village
Gamoswaana
Malopowabojang
Lobatse
Skilpadshek
Straatdrif
Mabaalstad
Lenong Lookouts
Sun C
Boshoek
Mogojwagojwe
Digawana
Blairbeth
Kromellenboog Dam
Skuinsdrif
Riekertsdam
Lindleyspoort
Mmathethe
Gathwane
Good Hope
Pisane Siding
Marico Bosveld Nature Reserve
Rusverby
Metlobo
Mokgomane
Bewley
Zeerust
Woodbine
Groot-Marico
Millvale
Rustenb
Sekhutlane River
Ramatlabama
Ottoshoop
Slurry
Wondereem
Swartruggens
Moloporivier
Pitshane
Makgobistad
Phitshane
Ramatlabama River
Carlsonia
Mmabatho
Mafikeng
Rooigrond
Elandsputte
Grasfontein
Bakerville
Mabaalstad
Koster
Vergelee
Mabule
Labera
Tshidilamolomo
Lotlamoreng Cultural Village
Grootpan
Merindol
Swartplaa
Gemsbokvlakte
Logageng
Itsoseng
Piet Plessis
Mosita
Lichtenburg
Klerkskra
Mooifontein
Harts River
Setlagole
Coligny
Ventersdorp
Madibogo
Deelpan
Biesiesvlei
Gerdau
Bodenstein
Makokskraal
Dovesdale
Mesa
Ganyesa
Stella
Geysdorp
Sannieshof
Vermaas
Haupstrus
Potchefstroom
Kameel
Barberspan
Bospoort
Brakspruit
Devonlea
Delareyville
Hartbeesfontein
Stilfontein
New Macha
Broedersput
Rostrataville
Ottosdal
Klerksdorp
Orkney
Migdol
Renosterspruit
Vryburg
Klein-Tswaing
Louwna
Strydpoort
Vierfontein
Amalia
Schweizer-Reneke
Wolmaransstad
Witpoort
Harrisburg
Mirage
Viljoenskro
Lykso
Koosfontein
Broadbent's Mission
Makwassie
Leeudoringstad
Steekdorings
Salpeterpan
Pudimoe
Avondstert
Boskuil
Kingswood
Bothaville
Reivilo
Manthestad
Taung
Bloemhof
Bloemhof Dam Nature Reserve
Maok
Kroonst
Blesmanspos
Pampierstad
Hartswater
Sandveld Nature Reserve
Winkelpos
Allanridge

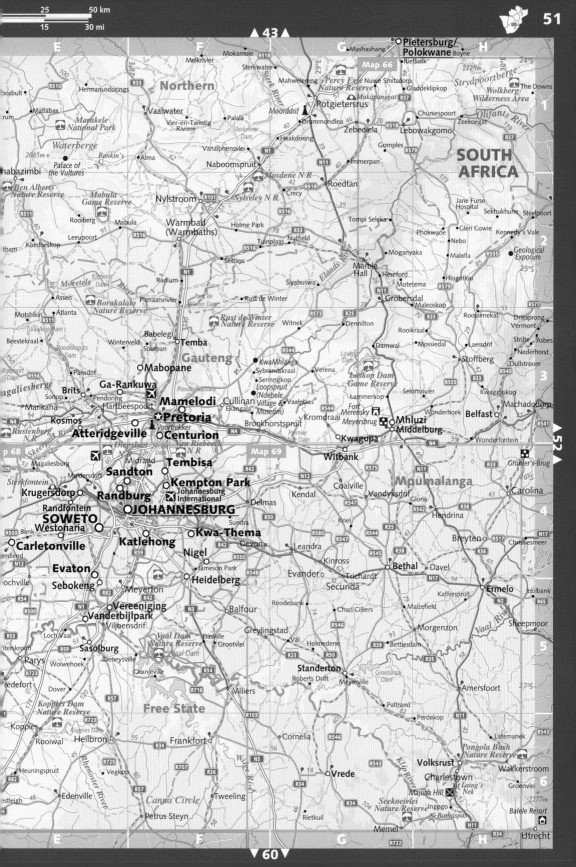

▲ 44 ▶

▼ 61 ▼

◀ 51 ▲

Map labels

Map 66

Northern

24°S

Lekgalameetse Nature Reserve
The Downs
Ofcolaco
Trichardtsdal
Klein Drakensburg
Olifants
Penge
Apiesdoring
Burgersfort
Steelpoort
Morone
Buffelsvlei
Maartenshoop
25°S
Graan
Mac-Mac
Potloodspruit
Lydenburg
Long Tom
Sabie
Klipsteen
Bultkop
Vermont
Asbes
Klipskool
Strilte
Nederhorst
Kwena Dam
Shoemanskloof
Montrose
Rivulets
Schoemanskloof
Waterval-Boven
Machadodorp
R541
Sewefontein
Bothasnek
Nelshoogte
Grobler's-Brug
26°S
Badplaas
Songimvelo Nature Reserve
Warburton
Chrissiesmeer
Lothair
Holbank
Bankkop
Amsterdam
Sheepmoor
Panbult
Iswepe
Piet Retief
Anysspruit
Wittenberg
Dirkiesdorp
Bergen
27°S
Grootspruit
Paulpietersburg
2277m
Balele Resort
Utrecht
Zungwini
Mpemvana
Hlobane
Ngobeni

R37
R36
R555
R532
R527
R531
R526
R36
R37
R577
R38
N17
R33
N2
R65
R543
R34

Bergpunt
Ohrigstad
Pilgrim's Rest
Graskop
Mogaba
Longsight
Branddraai
Blyde River Canyon N R
Hoedspruit
Abel Erasmus
River

Namakgale
Phalaborwa
Cycad Reserve
Mica
Klaserie Private Nature Reserve
Umbabat Game Reserve
Kampersrus
Klaserie
Acornhoek
Cottondale
Manyaleti Private Game Reserve
Sand River
Newington
Marite
Hazyview
Numbi
Napi
Paul Kruger
Kruger National Park
Nevu (666m)
Afsaal
Mthethomusha Game Reserve
Crocodile River
Nelspruit
Krokodilpoort
Kaapsehoop
Entre Nous
Althorpe
Louws Creek
Noordkaap
Louieville
Caledonian
Jeppe's Reef
Barberton
Saddleback
Phophonyane
Bulembu
Piggs Peak
Herefords
Jacks
St Peregrines
Bholekane
Lubuyane
Forbes Reef
Hhohho
Croydon
Hawane N R
Mission
Mbabane
Milwane Wildlife Sanctuary
Mhlambanyatsi
Bhunya
Matsapha International
Manzini
Mankayane
SWAZILAND
Mgazini
Sicunusa
Gege
Hlathikulu
Mooihoek
Maloma
Nhlangano
Shiselweni
Mhlosheni
Sihlutse (Hluthi)
Commondale
Luneberg
Pongola Bush Nature Reserve
Itala Game Reserve
Pongola
Louwsburg
Candover
Jozini
Ubombo
Mkuze
Mahlangasi
Mkuzi Game Reserve

Timbavati
Tshokwane
Trichardt Memorial
N'Wanetsi (Private)
Sweni River
Lindanda
Mapulanguene
Macaene
Machatuine
Ressano Garcia
Komatipoort
Crocodile Bridge
Hectorspruit
Tenbosch
Sabie
Rio Sabie
Chinhanguanine
Vundiça
Moamba
Pessene
Machaya
Namaacha
Mhlume
Matola
Boane
Catembe
Maputo
Maputo International
Marracuene
Costa do Sol
Ponta de Macaneta
Maphiveni
Mlawula N R
Goba
Simunye
Mhlumeni
Changalane
Porto Henrique
Bela Vista
Baia de Maputo
Cabo de Santa Maria
Inhaca
Ilha de Inh
Lago Maundo
Reserva Especial de Maputo
Lago Piti
Salamanga
Siteki
Palata
Nyetane Dam
Tikhuba
Sifunga Dam
Hendrick van Eck Dam
Big Bend
Mambane
Catuane
Manhoca
Zitundo
Ponta do Ouro
Kosi Bay
Kosi Bay N R
Lake Kosi
Boteler Point
Ndumo Game Reserve
Ndumo
Nsoko
Emangusi
Tembe Elephant Park
Ingwavuma
Lavumisa
Pongolapoort Public Resort Nature Reserve
Lake Sibaya
Lake Sibaya N R
Maputaland Marine Reserve
KwaZulu-Natal
Mbazwana
Mbabuleni
Sodwana Bay
Sodwana Bay National Park

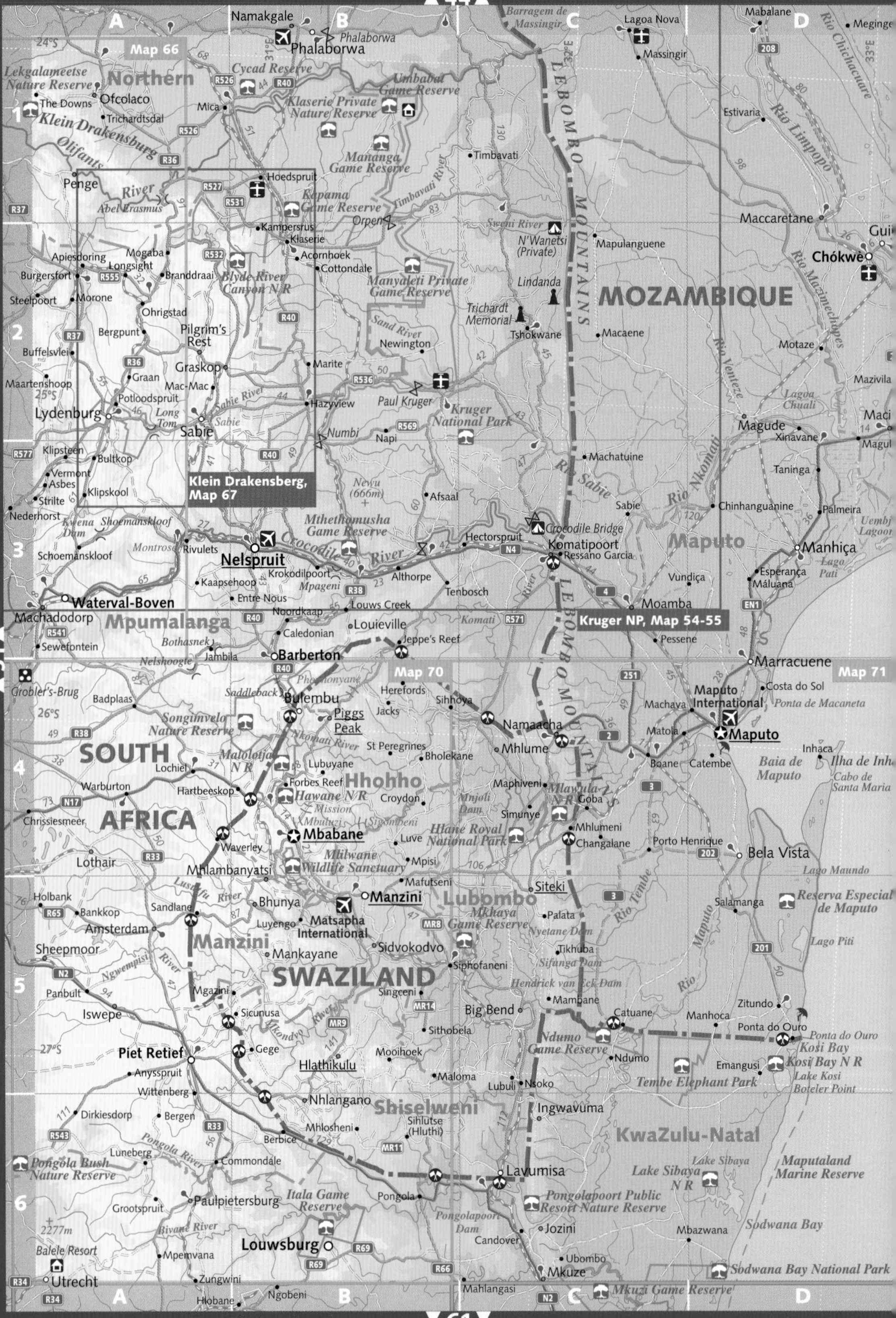

Lagoa Nova
Massingir
Barragem de Massingir
Mabalane
Meginge
Estivaria
Maccaretane
Gui
Chókwè
Rio Limpopo
Rio Macuenizhaes
Motaze
Mazivila
Maci
Magul
Taninga
Palmeira
Uembi Lagoor
Manhiça
Esperança
Máluana
Lago Pati
Magude
Xinavane
MAPUTO
Maputo
MOZAMBIQUE
LEBOMBO MOUNTAINS
LEBOMBO MOUNTAINS

SOUTH AFRICA
Mpumalanga
Manzini
Lubombo
Mkhaya Game Reserve
Singceni
Sithobela
Sidvokodvo
Mpisi
Mafutseni
Luyenga
Waverley
Hartbeeskop
Lochiel
Malolotja N R
Nkomati River
Sandlane
Lusutfu River

Numbers/roads: R526, R527, R531, R532, R533, R536, R527, R38, R40, R569, R571, R572, R40, N4, N2, EN1, 208, 202, 201, 251, MR8, MR9, MR11, MR14, R69, R66

Map 67 — Klein Drakensberg, Map 67

Map 70

Map 71

Kruger NP, Map 54-55

0   25   50 km
0   15   30 mi

E   **F**   **G**   **H**

34°E   35°E   36°E

Pembe

Lago
Nhavarre

Baía de
Inhambane

Maxixe   Barra   Ponta da Barra

Homoíne   Praia do Tofo

✚ **Inhambane**

Nalázi

Panda   Lindela   Baia dos Cocos

Maqueze   Jangamo   Praia de Jangamo

Inhambane   Cumbana   *Pandane*

Vila Gomes   Lago
da Costa   Nhadimbe

24°S   **1**

Marão   Lago
Nhangela

Gaza   Coguno   Chacane

Fumane   Maalamba

Chicomo   Inharrime

Mohambe   Helene   Závora   *Ponta de Závora*

adragoa   Chibuto   Chiducuane   Guilundo   Praia de Závora

EN1   **Manjacaze**   Lago   Lago
Chaimite   Marrangua   Poelela

cuane   Jantingue   254   EN1

Zandamela   Quissico   Lago
Maiene

Chissano   Lago
Chidenguele   Madender   Quissico

Chonguene

la   Lago
Nhanzume

Xai-Xai   Lago
Inhampavala

Praia do Chonguene
Praia do Xai-Xai

Zongoene
Zongoene

Lago Uembje

Praia do Bilene

25°S   **3**

I N D I A N   O C E A N

26°S   **4**

27°S   **6**

E   **F**   **G**   **H**

2

5

Rio Changane

Inhambane

▲ 44 ▲

A   B   C   D

1

Rio Chitolo

Rio Zebo chua

Combomune

Rio Limpopo

Mepuze

Muzamane

São Jorge do Limpopo

Rio 32°E

Gaza

MOZAMBIQUE

2

R200

Rio

Mapai

Nuanetsi

Rio

Singuedxi

Barragem de Massingir

Rio

3

Letaba

Shingwedzi

Mooiplaas

Sengwe

Pafuri

Babalala

Mopani

105

River

Letaba River

ZIMBABWE

River

Pafuri

57

Sirheni

Bateleur

Boulders (Private)

Shimuwini

44

Luvuvhu

Hlamalala River

River

River

River

KRUGER

Letaba

4

Waller's 31°E

Nyalaland Walking Trail Base Camp

Punda Maria

River

Mphongolo

River

Phugwane

Shingwedzi

NATIONAL

PARK

Lulekani

Phalaborwa

Thulamela Palace

39

Punda Maria

River

Namakgale

Masisi

River

R524

Pafuri

Nsama River

Nkomo

Hans Merensky Nature Reserve

River

Groot Letaba

5

Muale

River

Sagole Spa

Big Baobab Tree

Thathe-Vondo (Sacred Forest)

Mphaphuli Cycad Reserve

O Thohoyandou

Nsama Dam

Mineral Springs

Mulati

La Cotte

Murchison

Tsungane Fortress

Matavhelo

Mavamba

Giyani

River

Hildreth Ridge

34

Nikarhbak

Letsitele

R523

R81

R81

R529

Mineral Springs

Limpopo

Nwaedi

River

Mutale

Luphephe Dam

Tshitovhohoivhu

Lake Fundudzi

Iron-Age Furnace

Northern

River

66

Klein

Modjadji Nature Reserve

Ga-Modjadji

6

R525

Nwanedi National Park

Nzhelele Dam

Nwanedi Dam

Hannet Nature Reserve

Phiphidi

Mutshindudi

Sibasa

Tshakhuma

Tshiheni

Tshiheni

Klein Letaba

Letaba

River

River

SOUTH AFRICA

Ha-Magoro

Mamalla

Duiwelskloof

Tzaneen Dam

Tzaneen

Messina Nature Reserve

Tshipise

Dzata

R523

Mphephu Resort

Ratombo

Levubu

Elim Hospital

River Borders

R578

R579

R71

Mooketsi

Politsi

R36

O Messina 36

R525

R525

Nzhelele Dam

40

35

50

R81

36

23

Levubu

25

25°S

▼ 44 ▼

A   B   C   D

▲ 46 ▲   ▲ 47 ▲

Black Rock ● Bogenfels
+ Klinghardtsberg

DIAMOND AREA I
(Sperrgebiet)
RESTRICTED ACCESS

Rooiberg
+ (1121m)

Plumpudding Island
Sinclair's Island

Klinghardtsberg

Boegoeberg
+ (502m)

Chamais Bay

Witputs

Karas

Hunsberge

Fish River
Canyon
National Park

C13

Rosh Pinah

Ai Ais Hot
Springs Resort

Selingsdrif ● Selingsdrif

Jakkalsberge

River

Orange

Richtersveld
National Park

● Khubus

Gamkab River

Road Closed to Public

Oranjemund

Alexander Bay

Alexander Bay

Peace of
Paradise   Kotzel

Noordoewer
Vioolsdri

Holoat River

Eksteenfontein ●

● Lekkersing

3

29°S

Wreck Point

Cliff Point

Port Nolloth

McDougall's Bay

93

R382

Aninauspo

Wedge Point

Nigramoep

R355   94

Buffels River

ATLANTIC OCEAN

Grootmis ●   Kleinsee

Melkbospunt

4

30°S

Soebatsfont

Skulpfonteinpunt   Koiingnaas

Hondeklipbaai

Wallekraal

Strandfonteinpunt

5

31°S

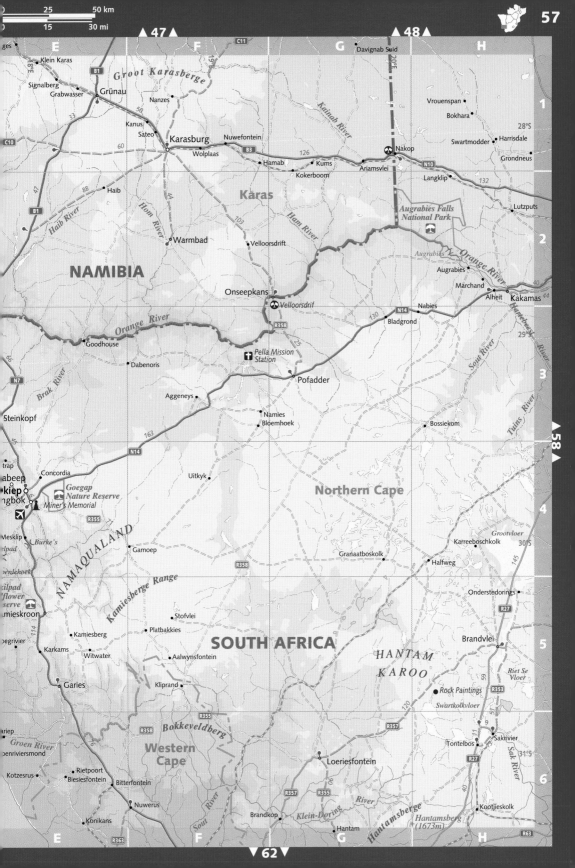

▲ 48 ▲   ▲ 49 ▲

	A	B	C	D

21°E

R360

Grondneus
Gelukspruit

28°S

Northern Cape

Moeswal
Langkloof
Olifantshoek
Vroeggedeel

Kathu
Sishen
Dingleton

29
54

Lohatlha

R31
Be

1855m +
Wonderwerk

Kuruman Hi

Danielsku

R385

Owendale   14
Lime Acres   48
Silver Str

R386
R385

Asbesberge

Pap
77
R385

Spitskop
Nature Reserve

Upington

Karos
Dagbreek

R10

120

160

N14

Langberge

Postmasburg
Bermolli

49

Koegelbeen

Campbell
48

80

Louisvale
Grootdrink
Kalkwerf

Kanoneiland

Keimoes
R359
Neilersdrif

Orange River

Matsap

64

Griekwastad
(Griquatown)

16

Douglas
Bucklands

Wegdraai
R64
Skerpioenpunt

Groblershoop
Boegoeberg
68

20

R64

R.

Kleinbegin

59

Koegrabie

R10

Volop

104

104

R383

R386

Higg's Hope
R357

29°S

Hartebeest River

R27

77

Tuins River

Putsonderwater

37

71
R383

Koegas
Westerberg

Nieketkshoop

94

Kenhardt

Rooiberg Dam

Marydale
Draghoender

100

142

Fransenhof

Prieska
36

14

R369

R361

Diemansputs

Prieskapoort

32

66

90

R387
12

Verneuk Pan

30°S

Copperton

Strydenburg

Grootvloer

Zwartkop

R357

R386

114

R403

N10

100

Omdraaisvlei
Sodium

N12

76

Onderstedorings

R357

150

Van Wyksvlei

136

88

Houtwaterdam

Riet Se Vloer

**SOUTH
AFRICA**

Bushman
Paintings
Vosburg

Giesenskraal
60

52

Britstown

R384

R361

R384

Volstruispoort

+ 1511m

90

*Smart
Syndicate*

Groen River

Corbelled Houses

Kareebospoort

R63

Carnarvon

Pampoenpoort

R403

R398

31°S

Sak River

128

Sterling

61

R63

R63

Merriman
De Klerk

Sfekaar

N12

Oingers River

Brakpoort

R63
Williston

Victoria West
Meltonwold

80

◄ 57 ◄

▲ 51 ▲

◄ 59 ►

A   **B**   **C**   **D**

Kroonstad
R713
Map 74
Geneva
Wonderkop
Petrus Steyn
Reitz
Memel
Newcas
R34
N3
R722
28°S
R34
Hennenman
N1
R76
Lindley
Liebenberg's Vlei
Warden
Cornelis River
Verkykerskop
Mullers
Chelmsford Dam
Nature Reserve
R70
R720
Steynsrus
Arlington
Danielsrus
R57
Molen River
Wilge River
Mt Everest
Game Reserve
Chelms
Virginia
Ventersburg
Valsrivier
R707
Bohlakong
Bothasberg
Bushman
Paintings
Platber
Collins
Welgeleë
R73
R26
Bethlehem
Saulspoort Dam
Botha
Harrismith
De Beers
Van Reenen
Van Reenen's
Allemanskraal Dam
Libertas
Senekal
Paul Roux
Kestell
Pretoriuskloof
Nature Reserve
Noupoortsnek
QwaQwa
Highland
National Park
Sterkfontein Dam
Sterkfontein Dam N R
Ladysmith
Willem Pretorius
Game Reserve
R70
Rooiberg
Rossb
Winburg
N5
R707
Rosendal
Clarens
Golden Gate
Highlands
National Park
Phuthaditjhaba
QwaQwa
Conservation
Area
Oliversbek
Spioenkop
R616
Spioenkop N R
Colenso
Marquard
R708
Ficksburg
N R
Fouriesburg
Monantsa
Moteng
Tugela
Royal Natal
National Park
Bergville
Woodstock Dam
R600
R74
N3
R74
Blou
Won
R709
Allandale
Clocolan
Ficksburg
Leribe (Hlotse)
Butha-Buthe
Rustler's Valley
A1
Witsieshoek
Mountain Inn
Cathedral
Peak (3004m)
Hlambonja
Wilderness Area
Cathedral Peak
State Forest
Estcourt
Excelsior
Maputsoe
Peka
Butha-Buthe
Rampai's
Ha Lejone
Giant's Castle
Game Reserve
Ro
R703
Melkoatleng
A1
Phuthiatsana River
Leribe
Katse Dam
Maluti Mountains
Ha Lejone
Cathedral Peak (3009m)
Giant's Castle (3312m)
Injasuti Dome
Inpasui Dome
N R
Tweespruit
N8
Teyateyaneng
B23
Seshote
Methalaneng
Mokhotlong
Mokhotlong
DRAKENSBERG
THE NATAL
DRAKENSBERG
PARK
R709
Ladybrand
Berea
Central Berg
Senqu (Orange) River
Thabana-Ntlenyana (3482m)
Loteni
Nature Reserve
Leeuwriver Dam
Maseru
Moshoeshoe's
Mountain Fortress
Ha Baroana
Mohale Dam
God Help Me
A5
Mohkoabong
Linakaneng
Redi (3298m)
Mzinkulwana
Hobhouse
Moshoeshoe
International
A2
Cheche
A3
Thaba-Tseka
Taung
Sani Top
Sani
Caledon River
Maseru
Map 79
Thaba Putsoa
(3096m)
Lesobeng River
Mashai
Thaba-Tseka
Likhakeng River
Mashai River
Map 80
Wepener
R20
Mafeteng
Gates of Paradise
Thaba Putsoa
Maletsunyane
Sehonghong
LESOTHO
Matebeng
Himeville N R
R617
Mafeteng
Rock
Malealea
Paintings
Ketane
Senqu River
Qacha's Nek
Tsoelike River
Garden Castle
State Forest
Bushman's Nek
Underberg
Vanstadensrus
R26
Cannibal
Makhaleng River
Mohale's Hoek
A4
Tsoelike
Sehlabathebe
National Park
Kingscote
Donnybrook
Egmont Dam
30°S
Makhalengbrue
Mohale's Hoek
Chief Moorosi's
Mountain Fortress
Qacha's Nek
R617
Zastron
A2
Fort
Hartley
Rock Paintings
Mt Moorosi
(2356m)
Matatiele
Franklin
Eastern
Cape
Umzimkul
Rouxville
Quthing (Moyeni)
Sigoga
Cedarville
Mount
Currie N R
Herschel
R392
Quthing
Kinirapoort
R56
Colonanek
Kokstad
Harding
R58
Lady Grey
Lundean's Nek
Tele
Ben Macdhui
(3001m)
Naudesnek
Mount
Fletcher
Keneka River
Ntsizwa
Brooks Nek
Umtamvuna R
Kraai River
R392
Tiffindell
Avoca Peak
(2769m)
R393
Pitseng
Mzimvubu River
Tina River
Mount
Ayliff
R61
Biz
Vineyard
31°S
R392
Barkly East
R58
Tsisana River
Halcyon Drift
Moot River
Tabankulu
Mzimkulu River
Flagstaff
Mkambati N R
Jamestown
Clanville
Clifford
R58
SOUTH AFRICA
Ntywenka
Palmerton
Msikaba
R344
R396
Rossouw
Barkly Pass
Barkly
Maclear
Ugie
N2
R396
Tsitsa Bridge
R56
R61
Lusikisiki
Port Grosvenor
2127m
Dordrecht
Morristown
Elliot
Eastern Cape
Sidwadweni
Stoneyridge
Indwe
Calapas

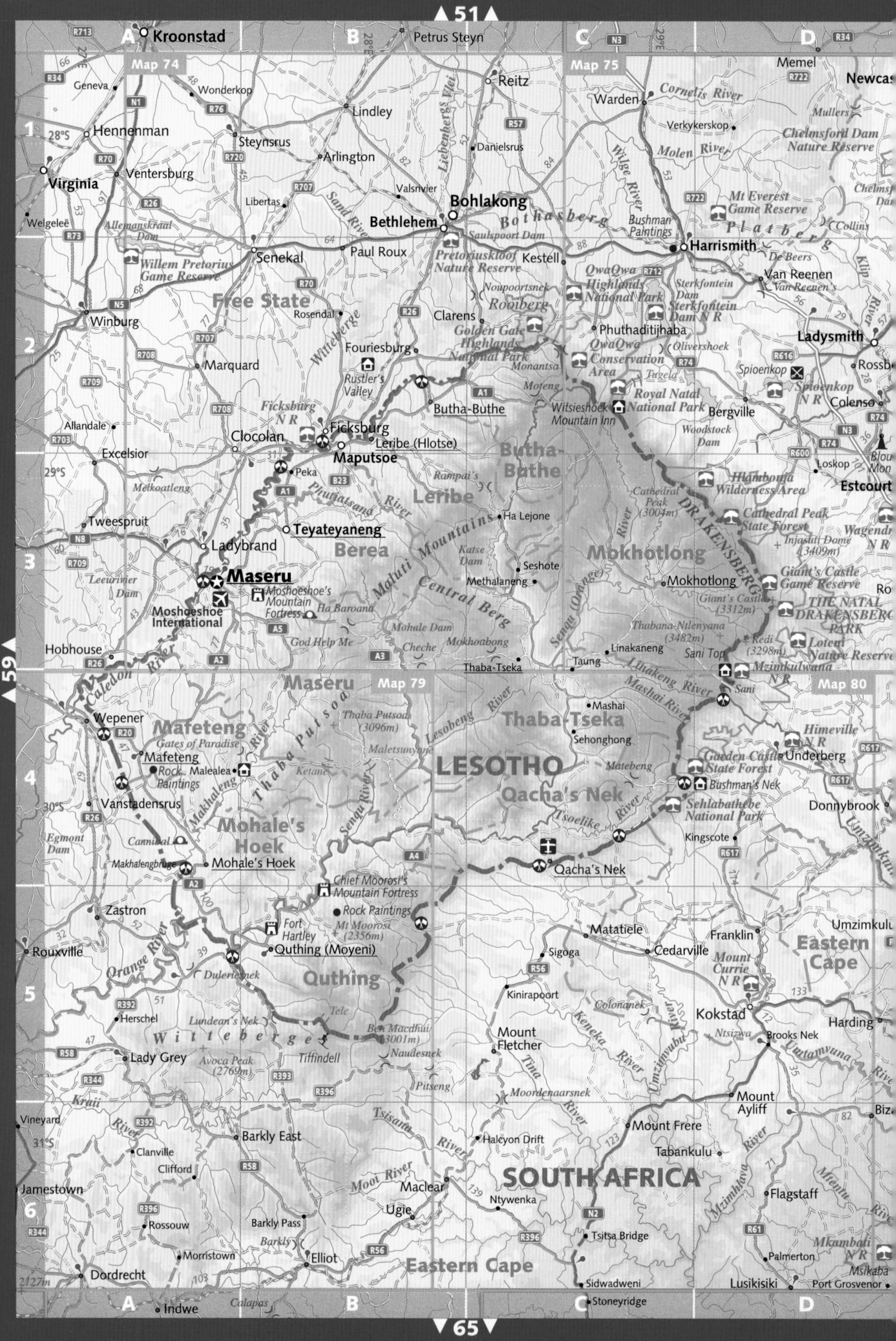

A   **B**   **C**   **D**

▲ **57** ▲

Map 82   Map 83

A   **B**   **C**   **D**

Konikans
Landplaas
R363
Koekenaap • Lutzville
Vredendal
Papendorp
Spruitdrif
Strandfontein
R362 R363
Doring Bay
Trawal
Heerenlogement
Rooiduine Point
Heerenlogement
Ratelfontein
32°S
Lambert's Bay
Wolfhuis
Graafwater
Leipoldtville
Sandberg
Baboon Point
Eland's Bay
Redelinghuys
R363
Ndoordkuil
R366
St Helena Bay
Stompneuspunt
Stompneusbaai
St Helena Bay
Dwarskersbos
Paternoster
Cape Columbine
Columbine
National Reserve
Laaiplek • Velddrif
Vredenburg
Bergrivier
Witwater
Berg River
Koringberg
Saldanha
R45
Hopefield

ATLANTIC OCEAN

Landbaan
Langebaan Lagoon
Churchhaven
West Coast National Park
Yzerfontein
Tienie Versveld Flower Reserve
Dassen Island
The Grotto Bay
R27
Bok Point
Bok Bay
Darling
R315
Mamre
R307
Kalbaskraal
Melkbosstrand
Robben Island
Table Bay
Milnerton
Clifton Beach
Camp's Bay
CAPE TOWN
Hout Bay
Hout Bay
Chapman's Bay
Kommetjie
Simon's Town
False Bay
Cape of Good Hope Nature Reserve
Cape of Good Hope
Olifantsbospunt
Buffels Bay
Cape Point
Cape Hangklip

Map 90   Map 91

Nieuwoudtville
Vanrhynspas
Oorlogskloof Nature Reserve
Knersvlakte
Soul River
R363
N7
R27
Vanrhynsdorp
Unionskraal
Klawer
Olifants River
R363
R364
Clanwilliam
Clanwilliam Dam
Pakhuis
Cederberg Wilderness Area
Cederberge
Algeria
Cederberg
Paleisheuwel
Het Kruis
Citrusdal
Piekenierskloof
Middelberg
Eendekuil
Aurora
R399
Sauer
Pools
R365
Goedverwag
Piketberg
De Hoek
Porterville
R44
Olifants River
Piketberg
R303
Groot Winterhoek Wilderness Area
Groot Winterhoek (2078m)
Swartruggens
Doring River

Northern Cape
Brandkop
Hantam
Akkerendam N R
Hantamsberge
20°E
Calvinia
R355
R354
Doringbos
Die Bos
Uitspankraal
Bloukrans
Tankwa Karoo National Park
Roggeveldberge
Tweefontein
Bo Wadrif
Tankwa River
Verlatekl
Middelpos
Bonel
Fish River
Wuppertal

SOUTH AFRICA

R355
Bokfontein
R356
Western Cape

Sonberg (1800m)
Gydopas
Saronberg
Moorreesburg
R44
Rust
R311
Riebeek Wes
Riebeek Kasteel
Gouda
Tulbagh
Ceres N R
Voëlvlei
Ceres
Malmesbury
Wolseley
Hermon
Bothamskloof
Wellington
Windmill
Paarl Mountain N R
Paarl
Mbekweni
Rawsonville
Moordkuil
R60
Durbanville
Parow
Cape Town International
Stellenbosch
Villiersdorp
Mitchells Plain
Hottentots Holland N R
Muizenberg
Strand
Kalk Bay
Gordon's Bay
Fish Hoek
Grabouw
Elgin
Vredendal
Botrivier
Rooiels Bay
Pringle Bay
R44
Kleinmond
R320
Hawston
Hangklip
Onrus
Hermanus
Sanddown Bay
Walker Bay
Gansbaai
Danger Point
Sandy Point
Pearly Beach
Quoin Point

Verkeerdevlei Dam
Hex River
Hottentotskloof
Touws River
Zuurplaats
Pieter Me
Kragers (1344
Die Venster
70
55 15
Sybasberg (1902m)
Karoo National Botanic Garden
De Doorns
Matroosberg
Tunnel
Avondrust
Bloutoring
Waboomsberg (1428m)
N1
Worcester
Rooihoogte
Langklo
Boerboonfo
Kleinbers (1115m)
Burgers
Montagu
Robertson
Nuy
Huguenot Toll Tunnel
Hammanshof
R43
Jonaskop (1646m)
Vrolijkheid N R
McGregor
Boschendal
Franschhoek
Berea
Pilaarkop (1655m)
Ashton
R62
Bonnievale
Marloth N R
Swellendam
Greyton
R406
Lindeshof
Stormsvlei
Swartberg (1089m)
Riviersonderend
R317
Rietpoel
Caledon
R326
Oukraal
Klipdale
Protem
Fairfield
Napier
De Hoop Vlei
Stanford
Papiesvlei
Salmonsdam N R
Baardskeerdersbos
Viljoenshof
Elim
Waenhuis (Arniston)
Struis Po
R316
R319
Struis Bay
Bredasdorp
Skip
Hotagterklip
Struisbaai
L'Agulhas
Cape Agulhas

33°S
34°S

A   **B**   **C**   **D**

25   50 km
15   30 mi

E   **F**   **G**   **H**

Sterling
Villiston
Quaggasfontein
) (Poort
Riet River
Basters berge
Sak River
R63
Loxton
Brakpoort
Victoria West
81   Meltonwold
Hutchinson
Verster
N12
Map 84
Map 85
R361
R63
R356   Saaifontein
101   Corbelled House
R353
Fraserburg
Rosedene
Sneeukraal
Wagenaarskraal
Three Sisters
Murraysburg
R63
THE KAROO
Restvale
Nelspoort
Biesiespoort
N1
62   **1**

R356
Teekloof
Hondefontein
erland
kloof
120
Karoo National Park
Molteno
Rosesberg
Renosterkop
Karriega River
R61
2

Beaufort West
Droerivier
Leeuw River
75
N1
Letjiesbos
Salt River
154   **3**
Merweville
Leeugamka Dam
Luttig
Leeu Gamka
Kruidfontein
143
Witteberge
Wiegnaarspoort
Kaapse Poortjie
Eastern Cape
Rietbron
N9
33°S
Barvlei Dam
Koringplaas
40
Zwarts
Prince Albert Road
Seekoegat
Kommandokraal
Volstruisleegte
R407
N12
141.4m
Perdepoort

Buffels River
Dwyka River
Gamka River
84   Dwyka
Vleifontein
N1   Koup
141/4m
▲64▲

Laingsburg
Rooinek
Floriskraal Dam
Bosluiskloof
Prince Albert
Ouktoof Dam
Swartberg
Klaarstroom
R407
Willowmore
Buyspoort
R407
Nuwekloof
Map 92
Map 93
R323
nysberg (1623m)
Seweweekspoort
Seweweekspoort
Gamkapoort Dam
Rouxpos
Zoar
96
Matjesrivier
Kruisrivier
R328
Grootkraal
Meiringspoort
Ghwarriespoort   34
R407
Kougaberge
Kouga River
R62
Kraaldorings
Schoemanspoort
Schoemanshoek
De Rust
Olifants River
75
R341
N9
R339
Zaaimansdal
Louterwater
Ladismith   17
Huisrivier
Calitzdorp
Oosgam
De Hoop
Oudtshoorn
Dysselsdorp
Kammanassieberge
Koutjie
Buffelsdrif
Uniondale
Avontuur
Haarlem
Joubertina
LITTLE KAROO
Rooiberg
Van Wyksdorp
Volmoed
N12
Kammanassie Dam
71
Molenrivier
Speelmans Kraal
De Vlug
Tsitsikammaberge
Plathuis
Jakatsfontein (1352m)
Warmwaterberg
Groot River
Robinson
Outeniqua
Herold
Wilderness N P
Daskop
Noll
Prince Alfred's
Keurbooms N R
Nature's Valley
The Crags
Kougaberge
moenshoek
Tradouw (1364m)
R323
Barrydale
Brandrivier
Langeberg
Garcias)
Cloetes
Ruitersbos
Sinksabrug
Kleinplaat
George
Wilderness
Knysna Nat'l Lake Area
Wittedrift
Robberg Nature & Marine Reserve
Plettenberg Bay
Cape Seal
Tradouw
R327
Langberg
Du Plessis
Brandwag
Herbertsdale
Herold's Bay
Pacaltsdorp
Goukamma N R
Knysna
The Heads
Brenton-on-sea
Heidelberg
Riversdale
N2
Hartenbos
N2
Groot Brakrivier
Mosselbaai
Buffalo Bay
Walker Point
Askraal
93
Danabaai
Mosselbaai
Vis Bay
R322
Albertinia
Droëvlakte
Riethuiskraal
Vermaaklikheid
Johnson's Post
Stilbaai-Oos
Vleesbaai
Cape Vacca (Kanonpunt)
Gouritsmond
R324
Whitesands
Infanta-on-River
Stilbaai-Wes
Groot Jongensfontein
St Sebastian Bay
Cape Barracouta
Cape Infanta
Elandspad

INDIAN OCEAN   **6**

35°S

E   **F**   **G**   **H**

▲ 59 ▲

Northern Cape

Richmond

Map 86

Sherborne

Middelburg

Rosmead

Map 87

Molteno
(Nomonde)

Syfergat

R398 709

R56

R391

Boesmanshoek

Sterkstroom

Heydon

Tafelberg

R390

Hofmeyr

Sneeuberg

Witkransnek

R401

Bailey

Bamboesberg

SOUTH AFRIC

Conway

Teviot

Grassridge
Dam

R390

R401

R344

Bowker's Park

Nieu-Bethesda

Bethesdaweg

Wapadsberg

Spitskopvlei

R388

Lootsberg

108

R61

R344

R61

Queens

Baroda

Tarkastad

Kamastone

Murraysburg

Naudesberg

Agter
Sneeuberg

N10

Sada

Whi

63

32°S

104

Van Ryneveld's
Pass Dam

Post
Chalmers

Cradock

Tsolwana
Game Reserve

**Western
Cape**

Ouberg

Karoo
N R

Bankberg

Halesowen

Elandsdrif

Spring Valley

Petersburg

Mountain
Zebra
N P

R390

Lake
Arthur

Winterberg

Waterdo

Devils
Bellows
Nek

**Graaff-
Reinet**

Munnikspoort

Swaershoekpas

Mortimer

Cameron's Glen

Seymour

Valley of Desolation

Drennan

Glenrock

54

R63

Swaershoek

Daggaboersnek

R344

Liddleton

Mpo
Gam
Rese
For

Aberdeen

Kendrew

Sandays River

R75

Witmos

Bedford

Blinkwater

N9

R338

733

R337

Pearston

Fish

Adelaide

R400

80

**Fort
Beaufort**

Martel
Tower

Aberdeen Road

R337

Eastern Cape

Cookhouse

R350

Double Drift
Game Reserve

Oatlands

Soutpansnek

**Somerset
East**

Long Hope

Fort
Brown

Lek

33°S

Jansenville

Vogel River

Waterford

Middleton

Carlisle Bridge

R344

Great
Rive
Reser

Klipplaat

Sheldon

R335

Ecca

Miller

1450m

Greystone

N10

R400

R350

Groot River

Swanepoelspoort

Mount Stewart

Baroe

Darlington
Dam

Klipfontein

R337

Riebeek Oos

Fort Selwyn

63

R329

719

Map 94

Steytlerville

Zuurberg
National Park

Zuurberg

Map 95

Shamwar
Game Reserve

Grahamst

Wolwefontein

26

Groot River

Glenconnor

Kirkwood

Suurberg

Alicedale

Paterson

Salem

Bathurs

Baviaanskloofberge

Grootwinterhoekberge

Addo
Elephant
N P

R75

R335

Alexandria

Al

Studtis

R332

Cockscomb
(1759m)

Addo

Ncanaha

Springmount

Cornville

Kenton

Colekeplaas

Cambria

Tip Tree

Kougaberge

Smitskraal

Demistkraal

Coega

Cape Padrone

Bushma
River Mo

Kouga River

Kouga Dam

Patensie

Andrieskraal

Hankey

Uitenhage

Algoa Bay

Joubertina

157

Van Stadens
Wild Flower Reserve

105

Despatch

Hobie Beach

Kareedouw

Walmer

PORT ELIZABETH

Shipwreck Coa

Stormsrivier

Clarkson

N2

Witteklip
Sea View

Summerstrand

34°S

Tsitsikamma
Lodge

Humansdorp

Port
Elizabeth

Cape Recife

Fort Frederick

Tsitsikamma
Coastal
National Park

Jeffreys Bay

Aston Bay
Paradysstrand

St Francis Bay

Oyster Bay

Cape St Francis

Tsitsikamma Point

Cape St Francis

35°S

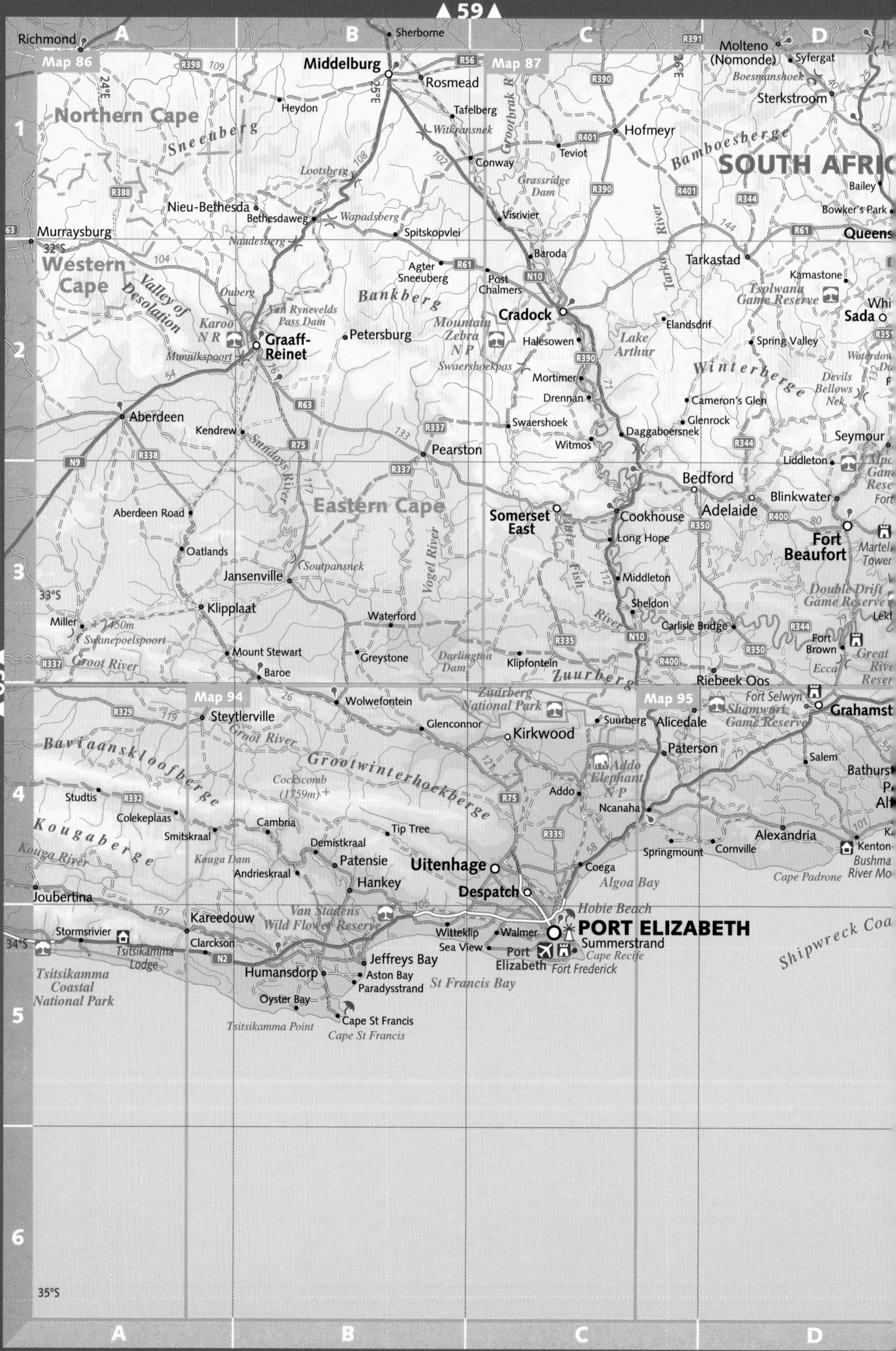

0 25 50 km
0 15 30 mi

▲ 60 ▲

Msikaba

E Dordrecht

Elliot **F** Ku-Mayima **G** Stoneyridge

Lusikisiki **H**

Cala Road

Qiba Calapas
Xalanga

Map 88

Umtata Dam
Luchaba
N R

Rock of
Execution 95

Mbotyi

Indwe

Garryowen
Cala

Satansnek

Ntibane

Umtata

Mlenganapas

Ntshilini Gemvale

Map 89

Braunville
132
Askeaton Lufuta Whitmore
Langdon
Coghlan
Nduli
N R

Libode

Old Bunting

Ntshilini

Port St Johns

1

Lady Frere

Southeyville Engcobo
Tsazo

All Saints Nek

Viedgesville Ngqeleni

Notintsila

Silaka Nature Reserve
The Kraal

Driver's Drift
Ncora Dam 218
Clarkebury

Bityi Qunu

Mqanduli
Ngqungqu

Old Morley

Hluleka Nature Reserve

Lubisi Dam

Ncora
Bashee Bridge

Munyu

Tshani
Coffee Bay

32°S

Konxa Dam
ibeleni

Nobokwe

Elliotdale (Xhora)

Wild Coast

Bolotwa Qamata
St Marks

R61 Cofimvaba

Hange Tsomo

Ntseshe

Colleywobbles

Alderley
Mpame

Mnewasa Point

Bacela
Xolobe

Idutywa

Cwebe Nature Reserve

2

aqu
Cathcart

Bellgrove

Nqamaqwe

Taleni

Ciko
Willowvale

The Haven
Dwesa Nature Reserve
Dwesa
Nqabara

Kologha
Forest Reserve
Stutterheim

Mgwali

Bolo
Reserve

N6
Bethel

Kei
Cuttings

Butterworth

Kentani

Qora Mouth
Mazeppa Bay

Gaika's
Grave

Ross

Komga
Prospect

Mpetu

Qolora Mouth
Kei Mouth
Morgan's Bay
Haga-Haga

Wavecrest

3

Kei Road

Quko

Braunschweig

Mpongo
Park

Tainton

Cape Henderson
Nature Reserve

King William's
Town
Zwelitsha

Bisho
Berlin
Potsdam

Beacon
Bay
Gonubie

Cintsa Bay

Mdantsane

Fort Murray

East London

Fort Murray
Punzana

Nahoon Reef

33°S

kfast Vlei

Kidd's Beach

Peddie

Bell
Wesley

Kiwane Resort

Hamburg

Bira River
Keiskama Point

Mpekweni Sun Marine Resort

Fish River Sun
Great Fish Point

4

INDIAN

OCEAN

34°S

5

35°S

6

E **F** **G** **H**

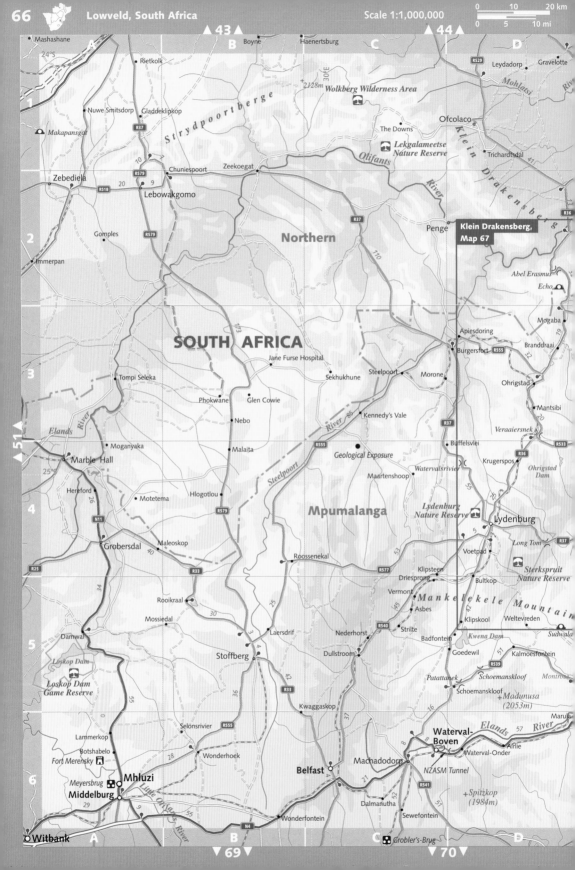

Klein Drakensberg, Map 67

Northern

SOUTH AFRICA

Mpumalanga

Wolkberg Wilderness Area

Lekgalameetse Nature Reserve

Loskop Dam Game Reserve

Lydenburg Nature Reserve

Sterkspruit Nature Reserve

Mankelekele Mountain

Mashashane
Rietkolk
Boyne
Haenertsburg
Leydadorp
Gravelotte
R529
Nuwe Smitsdorp
Gladdeklipkop
The Downs
Ofcolaco
Trichardtsdal
Makapansgat
Chuniespoort
Zeekoegat
Klein Drakensberg
Zebediela
Lebowakgomo
Penge
Gomples
Immerpan
Abel Erasmus
Echo
Mogaba
Branddraai
Jane Furse Hospital
Sekhukhune
Steelpoort
Apiesdoring
Burgersfort
R555
Tompi Seleka
Morone
Phokwane
Glen Cowie
Kennedy's Vale
Ohrigstad
Nebo
Mantsibi
Elands River
Malaita
Buffelsvlei
Veraaiersnek
R533
Marble Hall
Geological Exposure
Krugerspos
R36
Hereford
Maartenshoop
Watervalsrivier
Ohrigstad Dam
Motetema
Hlogotlou
Grobersdal
Maleoskop
Roossenekal
Lydenburg
Long Tom
R37
Voetpad
Klipsteen
Driesprong
Bultkop
Rooikraal
Vermont
Mossiedal
Asbes
Klipskool
Weltevreden
Damwal
Laersdrif
Nederhorst
Strilte
Kwena Dam
Sudwala
Stoffberg
Dullstroom
Badfontein
Goedewil
Kalmoesfontein
R539
Patattanek
Schoemanskloof
Montrose
Schoemanskloof
Madunusa (2053m)
Kwaggaskop
Marulu
Selonsrivier
R555
Wonderhoek
Waterval-Boven
Elands River
Aflrie
Lammerkop
Waterval-Onder
Botshabelo
Machadodorp
Fort Merensky
Meyersbrug
Mhluzi
Belfast
NZASM Tunnel
Middelburg
Dalmanutha
Spitzkop (1984m)
Witbank
Wonderfontein
Sewefontein
Grobler's-Brug

0   5   10 km
0   3   6 mi

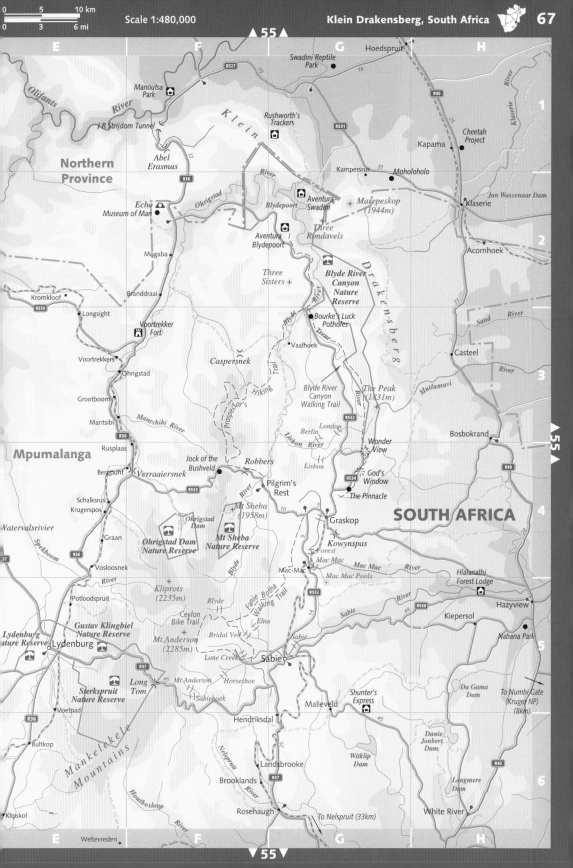

▲55▲

E   F   G   H

Hoedspruit

Swadini Reptile Park

R527

Olifants River

Manoutsa Park

J R Strijdom Tunnel

R531

R40

Kapama

Cheetah Project

1

Klaserie River

Klein

Rushworth's Trackers

Kampersrus

Moholoholo

Jan Wassenaar Dam

Klaserie

Northern Province

Abel Erasmus

River

R36

Ohrigstad

Aventura Swadini

Blydepoort

Makepeskop (1944m)

Echo Museum of Man

Aventura Blydepoort

Three Rondavels

Acornhoek

2

Mogaba

Three Sisters

Blyde River Canyon Nature Reserve

Drakensberg

Branddraai

Kromkloof

Longsight

Voortrekker Fort

Blyde River

Bourke's Luck Potholes

Sand River

R555

Casteel

Voortrekkers

Caspersnek

Vaalhoek

3

Ohrigstad

Grootboom

Mantsibi River

Hiking Trail

Prospector's

Blyde River Canyon Walking Trail

The Peak (1831m)

River

Mutlumuvi River

Bosbokrand

Mantsibi

R36

Rusplaas

Berlin

London

R532

Lisbon River

Wonder View

Mpumalanga

Bergpunt

Verraaiersnek

Jock of the Bushveld

Robbers

Lisbon

God's Window

R40

55▲

R533

Pilgrim's Rest

R534

The Pinnacle

4

Schalksrus

Krugerspos

Graan

Mt Sheba (1958m)

River

Blyde

10

5

Graskop

SOUTH AFRICA

Watervalsrivier

Ohrigstad Dam

Mt Sheba Nature Reserve

Kowynspas Forest

Spekboom

R36

Ohrigstad Dam Nature Reserve

Mac Mac

Mac Mac River

Vosloosnek

Mac-Mac

Mac Mac Pools

Hlalanathi Forest Lodge

Potloodspruit

Kliprots (2235m)

Blyde

Fanie Botha Walking Trail

R532

Sabie River

R536

Kiepersol

Hazyview

37

Ceylon Bike Trail

Elna

14

44

Lydenburg Nature Reserve

Gustav Klingbiel Nature Reserve

Lydenburg

Mt Anderson (2285m)

Bridal Veil

Sabie

Nabana Park

5

R37

Lone Creek

Sabie

Da Gama Dam

To Numbi Gate (Kruger NP) (8km)

Long Tom

Mt Anderson

Horseshoe

Shunter's Express

Sterkspruit Nature Reserve

Sabiehoek

Malieveld

45

Danie Joubert Dam

Voetpad

Hendriksdal

R36

Bultkop

Nelspruit River

Landsbrooke

Witklip Dam

Langmere Dam

Mankelekele Mountains

Brooklands

R37

R40

6

Klipskol

Houtbosloop River

Rosehaugh

To Nelspruit (33km)

White River

Weltevreden

E   F   G   H

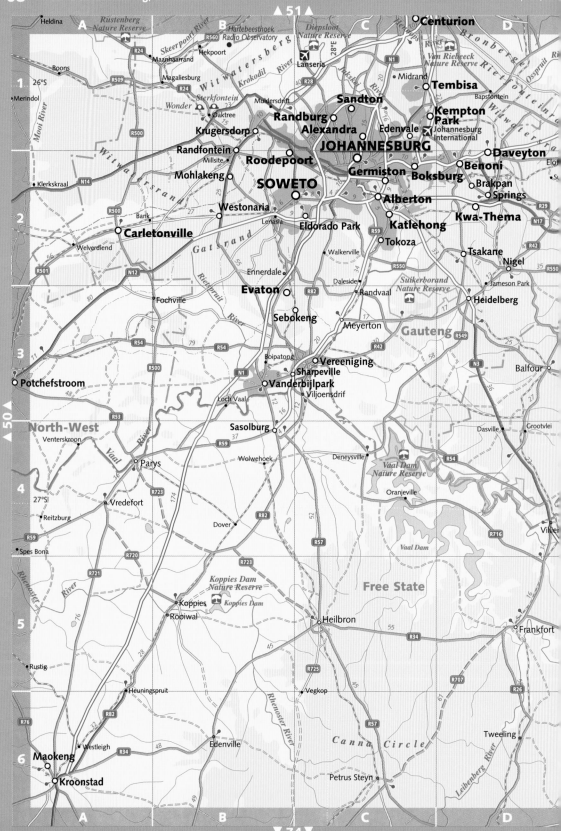

▲ 51 ▲

◄ 50 ▲

▼ 74 ▼

0 10 20 km
0 5 10 mi

E N4 Balmoral **Kwaguqa** F **G** Wonderfontein N4 **H** 30°E

Witbank Clewei
Klipfontein
R545 30
Bronkhorstspruit Dam
Nooitgedacht Dam
R33
92
47
10
R544
R575
26.5
26 Arbor N12 Minnar
Coalville
R547
N11
Carolina
Argent
Kendal Ogies
Vandyksdrif
43
Delmas
71
Gloria R542
R38
Hendrina
32
Little Olifants River

1

R50
14
R35
Kriel
26
R544
52
Hendrina 78
23
R517
Breyten

2

R580 R547 22
R35
R38 55
Devon 16 Leandra
20
R580
29
R545 11
54
R36
33
38
Kinross 16
Bethal
Davel
Ermelo

3

Evander
Trichardt
26
N17
Kaffersprult
Secunda
30
Roodebank
Maizefield
45
Charl Cilliers
R546
36
Mpumalanga
Morgenzon
31
59
R547
Vaal River

Val
Bettiesdam
R39
R35
70
Holmedene
R50
19
Grootdraai Dam
42

4

reylingstad
R23 54
Standerton
Meyerville
Roberts Drift
27°S

Vaal River
Waterval River

R103 60
Amersfoort
Cornelia
R546
Paltrand
N11
Perdekop
42
Latemanek
Pongola Bush Nature Reserve

5

R34
Volksrust 27 Wakkerstroom
82 R543
Charlestown
Groenvlei
Vrede
18
N3
R34
Balelesberg
Laingsnek
Majuba Hill ✕
53
R34 58
Ingogo
N11
Rietkuil
Seekoeivlei Nature Reserve
R34
Bothaspas
Memel

6

E F R722 **G** **H** R34

SOUTH AFRICA

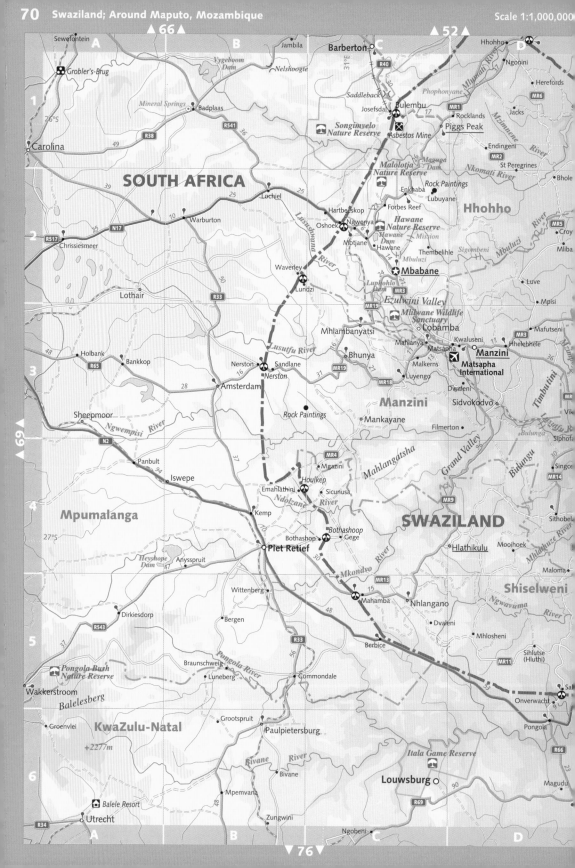

▲ 66 ▲   ▲ 52 ▲

Sewefontein

Grobler's-Brug

Carolina

26°S

R38

Mineral Springs

Badplaas

R541

SOUTH AFRICA

R517

Chrissiesmeer

N17

Warburton

Lochiel

Waverley

Lothair

R33

Lundzi

Holbank

R65

Bankkop

Nerston

Sandlane

Amsterdam

Nerston

Sheepmoor

Ngwempisi River

N2

Panbult

Iswepe

Mpumalanga

27°S

Heyshope Dam

Anysspruit

Piet Retief

Wittenberg

Bergen

Dirkiesdorp

R543

Braunschweig

Luneberg

Commondale

R33

Berbice

Pongola Bush Nature Reserve

Wakkerstroom

Balelesberg

Groenvlei

KwaZulu-Natal

+2277m

Grootspruit

Paulpietersburg

Bivane River

Bivane

Balele Resort

R34

Utrecht

Mpemvana

Zungwini

Jambila

Nelshoogte

Vygeboom Dam

Barberton

R40

Saddleback

Josefsdal

Bulembu

Songimvelo Nature Reserve

Asbestos Mine

Malolotja Nature Reserve

Enkhaba

Forbes Reef

Hartbeeskop

Ngwenya

Oshoek

Motjane

Mhlambanyatsi

Lusushwana River

Lusutfu River

Rock Paintings

Mankayane

Bhunya

MR19

Luyengo

MR4

Mgazini

Houlkep

Emahlathini

Sicunusa

Ndotzane

Kemp

River

Bothashoop

Bothashop

Gege

Mahamba

MR13

Mkondvo River

15

Nhlangano

Dvaleni

Mhlosheni

Pongola River

Bothashoop

Louwsburg

Itala Game Reserve

R69

Ngobeni

Hhohho

Ngonini

Herefords

MR6

Rocklands

MR1

Piggs Peak

Jacks

Rock Paintings

Lubuyane

Maguga Dam

Nkomati River

Endingeni

St Peregrines

Bhole

Hhohho

Hawane Nature Reserve

Hawane Dam

Hawane

Mission

Thembelihle

Mbuluzi

Sigombeni

Mbuluzi River

MR5

Croy

Mliba

Luphohlo Dam

Mbabane

MR3

MR19

Ezulwini Valley

Mlilwane Wildlife Sanctuary

Lobamba

Mahlanya

Matsapha

Kwaluseni

Manzini

Matsapha International

Malkerns

Hhelehhele

MR3

Mafutseni

Luve

Mpisi

Manzini

Dwaleni

Sidvokodvo

Timbutini

Vik

Mahlangatsha

Grand Valley

Bulunga

Bidungu

Singce

MR14

MR9

SWAZILAND

Sithobela

Mhlambuze River

Hlathikulu

Mooihoek

Maloma

Shiselweni

Ngwavuma River

MR11

Sihlutse (Hluthi)

Onverwacht

Pongola

Magudu

R66

▼ 76 ▼

0 10 20 km
0 5 10 mi

SOUTH AFRICA

R571

32°E
33°E

Marracuene
Complexo Turístico Macaneta
Costa do Sol
Ponta de Macaneta

49
251
28
38

Machava
15
Maputo International
7
14
MAPUTO
Ilha de Xefita Grande

Namaacha
Lomahasha
Namaacha
2
12
71
7
Boane
Matola
Catembe

Portuguese Island

Inhaca
Ilha de Inhaca

26°S

Vuvulane
MR24
Tambankulu
Maphiveni
Gate to Mlawula NR
Simunye
Goba
Goba Fronteira
Mhlumeni
Changalane

Barragem dos Pequenos Lebombos

3
Rio Tembe
35
37

Baia de Maputo
Cabo de Santa Maria

Mhlume
MR3
Injoli Dam
Puluzane River
MR3
Hlane Royal National Park
Mlawula & Mbuluzi Nature Reserves

24
10
Porto Henrique
202
Bela Vista

Lago Maundo

MOZAMBIQUE

Reserva Especial de Maputo (Maputo Elephant Reserve)

Lonhlupheko
Lukhula
Mpaka Station
Siteki
12
63

50
201
Salamanga

Lago Piti

Magomba
Palata
Nyetane Dam
Sifunga Dam
Tikhuba

Maputo

3

Ikhaya e Reserve
huzumoya
MR16
Usutu River
33

Hendrick van Eck Dam
Mambane

Rio Maputo

INDIAN OCEAN

Big Bend
Bridge washed out
Matata
Catuane
Manhoca
Zitundo
13
Ponta d'Ouro

Ndumo Game Reserve
Tembe Elephant Park
Ndumo
Kosi Bay Nature Reserve
Kosi Bay
Ponta d'Ouro

Nisela Safaris
Lubuli
Nsoko
Emangusi
Lake Kosi
Boteler Point

27°S

MAPUTALAND

MR8
Ingwavuma

SOUTH AFRICA

Coastal Forest Reserve

Maputaland Marine Reserve

Lavumisa
Golela
34
28

LEBOMBO MOUNTAINS

Pongola River

Lake Sibaya
Hully Point

Pongolapoort Dam
Pongolapoort Public Resort Nature Reserve
N2
Jozini

KwaZulu-Natal

Lake Sibaya Nature Reserve

Sodwana Bay

Candover
Ubombo
Mbazwana

R69
Mahlangasi
Mkuze
Mkuze River
Ghost Mountain (529m)
Mkuzi Game Reserve
Ozabeni State Forest
Sodwana Bay
Jesser Point
Sodwana Bay National Park

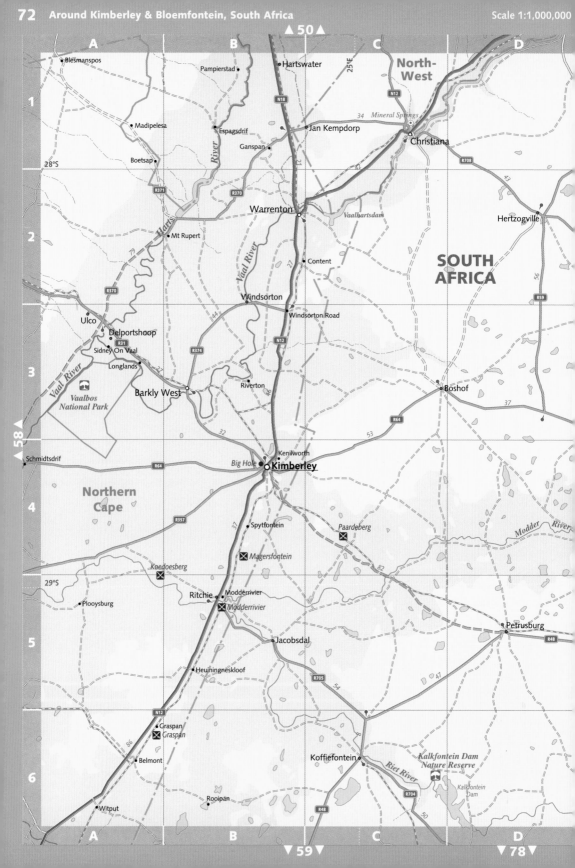

▲ 50 ▲

A **B** **C** **D**

Blesmanspos

Pampierstad

Hartswater

North-West

N18

25°E

N12

1

Madipelesa

Espagsdrif

Ganspan

Jan Kempdorp

34 Mineral Springs

Christiana

R708

Boetsap

28°S

R371

R370

River

Warrenton

Vaalhartsdam

Hertzogville

43

2

Harts

Mt Rupert

Vaal River

Content

SOUTH AFRICA

56

R59

R370

Windsorton

R31

144

Windsorton Road

N12

Ulco

Delportshoop

Sidney On Vaal

R374

3

Vaal River

Longlands

27

Riverton

Boshof

37

Vaalbos National Park

Barkly West

32

53

R64

▲ 58 ▲

Schmidtsdrif

R64

Big Hole

Kenilworth

Kimberley

Northern Cape

R357

4

37

Spytfontein

Paardeberg

Modder River

Magersfontein

82

Koedoesberg

29°S

Plooysburg

Ritchie

Modderrivier

Modderrivier

Petrusburg

R48

5

Jacobsdal

Heuiningneskloof

R705

54

47

N12

Graspan

Graspan

Koffiefontein

Kalkfontein Dam Nature Reserve

Kalkfontein Dam

Belmont

86

Riet River

R704

50

6

Rooipan

R48

Witput

A **B** **C** **D**

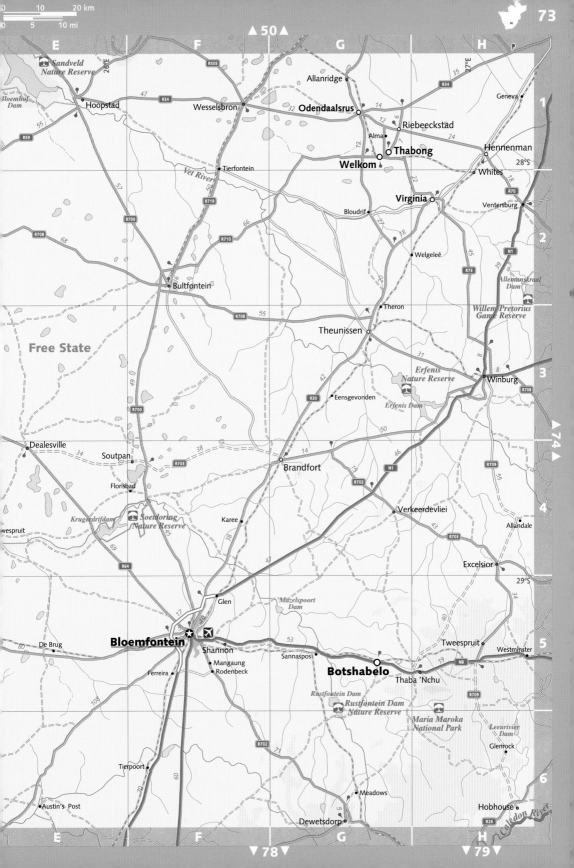

▲ 68 ▲

▲ 73 ▲

SOUTH AFRICA

Reitz

Geneva
Wonderkop
N1
Steynsrus
Ventersburg
Arlington
Lindley
R76
Danielsrus
R57
R720
R707
Libertas
Valsrivier
Kransfontein
R26
Bohlakong
Bethlehem
Saulspoort Dam
Senekal
Paul Roux
Pretoriuskloof Nature Reserve
N5
Allemanskraal Dam
Willem Pretorius Game Reserve
R26
Noupoortsnek
Rooiberge
Clarens
+2477m
Golden Gate Highlands National Park
Rustler's Valley
R707
Rosendal
Fouriesburg
Mohokare (Caledon) River
Sefa
Mon
R708
Marquard
Free State
Hendrick's Drift
Libono
Caledonspoort
Butha-Buthe
R70
Witteberge
Joel's Drift
Butha-Buthe
A1
Moteng
Moteng
Allandale
Jonathane
Dinosaur Footprints
Khabo
Pela-Tsoeu
Ficksburg
Ficksburg Nature Reserve
Leribe (Hlotse)
Malaoaneng
Lempha
Gumtree
Malibamat'so
Clocolan
Maputsoe
Dinosaur Footprints
Mahobong
Melkoatleng
Pekabrug
Corn Exchange
B25
Matlameng
+3277m
Liqhobo
Peka
Pitseng
Rampai's
Kao
A1
Kolonyama
Koeneng
Pelaneng
Westminster
N8
Rakoloi
Mamathe
Nokong
Leribe
Ha Lejone
Marseilles
Ladybrand
Tebetebeng
Mapoteng
Moletsane
Matsoku
Phutiatsana River
Katse Dam
Seshote
Berea
Sefikeng
Mateka
Berea
Kommissiepoort
Maserubrug
Maseru
Bethany
Moshoeshoe's Mountain Fortress
Thaba-Bosiu
Methalan
Masianokeng
Ha Baroana
Nazareth
Bushman's
Maluti Mountains
Bokong
Katse
Mazenod
Ha Ntsi
Machache
God Help Me
Central Berg
LESOTHO
Mantsebo
Ha Makhalanyane
Roma
Mofimo-Nthuse
Mohale Dam
Likalaneng
Mofoka
A5
Blue Mountain
Thaba-Tseka
Mohokare (Caledon) River
Kolo
A2
Ngope Ts'oeu
Makhaleng
A3
Marakabei
Mantsonyane
Mokhoabong
Thaba-Tseka
Palama
Monja
Matsieng
Tlali
Maseru
Cheche

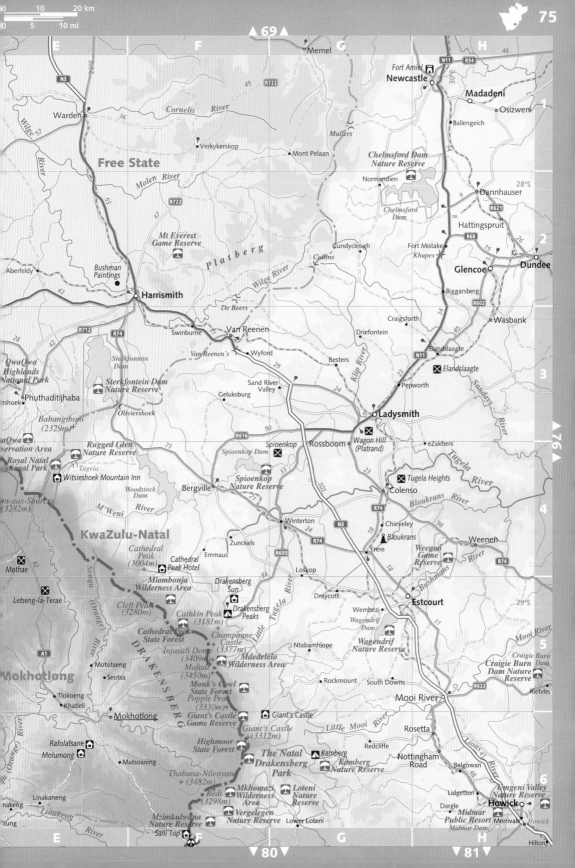

▲ 70 ▲

31°E

R34

A   **B**   **C**   **D**

Utrecht

Zungwini

Vryheid Nature Reserve

Kambule

Ngobeni

Hlobane

Alpha

Ntendeka Wilderness Area

R34

Blood River

Vryheid

Raadsaal & Fort of New Republic

Scheepersnek

Steilrand

23

Ngome

R618

R33

Bloedrivier

Kingsley

43

25

Mondlo

34

Swart Umfolozi

Black (Swart) Umfolozi River

26 43

Nongoma

R66

28°S

Calvert

Gluckstadt

SOUTH AFRICA

6

Ntabebomvu

53

Buffalo River

48

Blood River

Blood River

Prince Imperial Grave

Nondweni

Nhlazatshe

Mahlabatini

Dundee

Talana

52

Vant's Drift

R68

Nqutu

Fort Newdigate

Fort Nolela

Ulundi

39

Fort Northampton

59

Fort Marshall

R34

Ulundi

Rorke's Drift

Rorke's Drift

Isandlwana

Silutshana

R68

Babanango

White (Wit) Umfolozi River

21

Ondini

Fugitive's Drift

Helpmekaar

Elandskraal

Mangeni

Mgungundlovu (Retief's Grave)

50

Mtonjaneni

R33

14

Pomeroy

Qudeni

Osborn

Randalhurst

Melmoth

KwaZulu-Natal

27

Nkandla

Ndundulu

Nkwalini

R34

46

Tugela River

Dlolwana

Nsuze River

Site of Shaka's Kraal

Coward's Bush

Tugela Ferry

71

Z U L U L A N D

22

Keate's Drift

The Ranch

Cetshwayo's Grave

Entumeni Nature Reserve

R33

Entumeni

Eshowe

Kwa-Mondi Fort

Fort Nongqai

R74

Muden

Kranskop

Tugela River

21

Mtu

29°S

R74

Ahrens

R66

46

Mooi River

Craigie Burn Dam Nature Reserve

Craigie Burn Dam

Greytown

23

21

Kwa Sizabantu Mission

Amatikulu

Gingindlovu

Nyoni

N2

R622

Rietvlei

Fort Mtombeni

Mapumulo

Tugela

Battle of the Tugela

Mandini

103

Sevenoaks

37

Otimati

Newark

The Ultimatum Tree

Tugela Mouth

Umvoti River

43

Fort Pearson

R74

York

New Hanover

30

Fawnleas

Darnall

11

Albert Falls Dam

Dalton

62

New Guelderland

Umgeni Valley Nature Reserve

Mpolweni

Wartburg

41

Shaka's

Stanger

Zinkwazi

Dolphin Coast

Albert Falls

Blythdale

Howick

Albert Falls Nature Reserve

Aldinville

Merrivale

Queen Elizabeth Park

Shakaskraal

Sheffield

Hilton

Umhlali

Salt Rock

Sheffield Beach

25

75

75

▼ 81 ▼

Ndwedwe

0 10   20 km
0   5   10 mi

E **F** **G** **H**

Mahlangasi

Mkuze

Mkuze River

Ghost Mountain
(529m)

Mkuzi Game
Reserve

Sodwana Bay
National Park

Phinda Resource
Reserve

Greater
St Lucia
Wetlands

Mkuze River

Mkuze
Swamp

Mzinene River

St Lucia Marine Reserve

1

Msunduzi River

N2

32°E

33°E

False
Bay Park

Leven Point

False Bay

Lake St Lucia

Bird Island

Lane Island

Hilltop

Memorial

Hluhluwe

Dugandlovu

Tewati Wilderness Area

28°S

2

Hlabisa

*Thiyeni
Waterhole*

Hluhluwe

Hluhluwe Dam

Dumazulu Cultural
Village

Fannies Island

Cape Vidal

Lake
Bangazi

Bhangazi

R618

Hluhluwe-
Umfolozi
Park

Gunjaneni

Charters Creek

Black

Mpila

Mambeni

Nyalazi River

Somkele

Makakatane

Catalina
Bay

St Lucia
Game Reserve

Mission Rocks

3

*Mphafa
Waterhole*

Umfolozi

Swart

47

Dukuduku
Forest

R618

Mhlatuze
State Forest

Mtubatuba

Riverview

Mapelane

Mapelane
Nature Reserve

St Lucia Resort

River

N2

Cape St Lucia

Red Hill
(175m)

Teza

4

KwaMbonambi

Mposa

Enseleni
Nature Reserve

*Nsezi
Lake*

angeni

*Mzingazi
Lake*

Richards Bay

elixton

*Ungpa
Lake*

*Mhlatuzi
Lagoon*

Richards Bay
Game Reserve

*Umlalazi
ure Reserve*

INDIAN OCEAN

29°S

5

6

E **F** **G** **H**

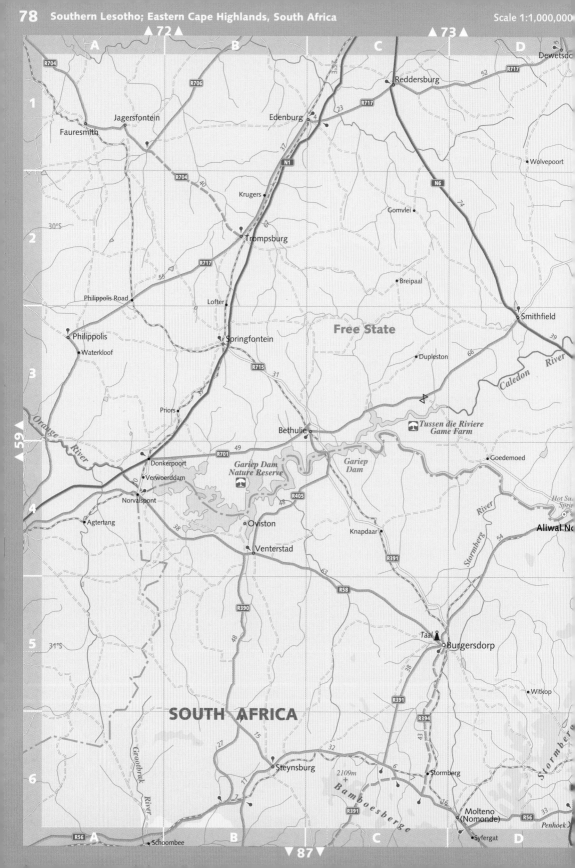

▲ 72 ▲   ▲ 73 ▲

A   B   C   D

R704

Dewetsdc

Jagersfontein
Fauresmith

R706

R717
Reddersburg

52

R717

Edenburg

23

R717

R704

N1

37

N6

74

Krugers

Gomvlei

Wolvepoort

30°S

Trompsburg

R717

55

Breipaal

Free State

Philippolis Road

Lofter

Smithfield

Philippolis

Springfontein

Dupleston

66

Caledon River

39

Waterkloof

R715

31

Priors

▲ 59 ▲

Orange River

Bethulie

Tussen die Riviere
Game Farm

R701

49

Gariep Dam
Nature Reserve

Gariep
Dam

Goedemoed

Donkerpoort

Verwoerddam

R405

48

River

Hot Su
Spri

Norvalspont

Agtertang

38

Oviston

Knapdaar

Stormberg River

54

Aliwal N

Venterstad

63

R391

R58

R390

48

Taal

Burgersdorp

31°S

R391

Witkop

R394

SOUTH AFRICA

27

15

32

43

Stormber

2109m

6

Steynsburg

17

Bamboesberge

Stormberg

76

Groothrek River

R391

Molteno
(Nomonde)

R56

Penhoek

R56   A   B   C   Syfergat   D

Schoombee

▼ 87 ▼

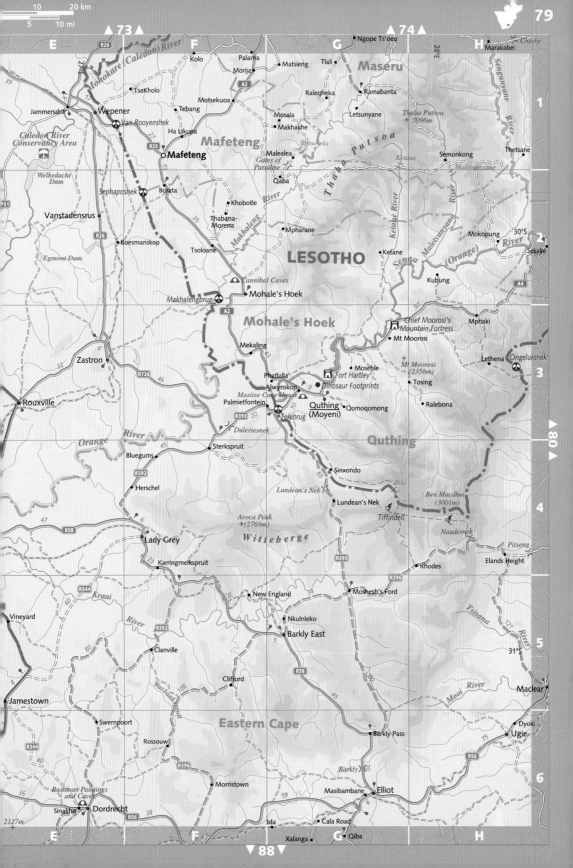

10   20 km
5   10 mi

E   F   G   H

Mohokare (Caledon) River
39
Jammersdrif
Wepener
Van Rooyenshek
TsaKholo
Kolo
Palama
Morija
Matsieng
Tlali
Ngope Ts'oeu
Marakabei
Cheche
Maseru
Raleqheka
Ramabanta
Thaba Putsoa
+ 3096m
Semonkong
Thetsane
Sengunyane River
28°E

1

Caledon River
Conservancy Area
Tebang
Ha Likupa
Motsekuoa
Mosala
Makhakhe
Letsunyane
Butsoela
Ketane
Maletsunyane River

Mafeteng
Mafeteng
Maleala
Gates of
Paradise
Qaba
Mpharane
Thaba Putsoa
Mokopung
30°S

2

Welbedacht
Dam
Sephaposhek
Borata
Khobotle
Thabana-
Morena
Makhaleng River
LESOTHO
Ketane
Kubung
Sengu (Orange) River
Sekake
A4

Vanstadensrus
Boesmanskop
Tsoloane
Cannibal Caves
Mohale's Hoek
Makhalengbrug
Egmont Dam
Chief Moorosi's
Mountain Fortress
Mphaki

3

Mohale's Hoek
Mekaling
Mt Moorosi
Mt Moorosi
(2356m)
Lethena
Ongeluksnek

Zastron
R726
Phatlalla
Alwynskop
Palmietfontein
Masitse Cave House
Telebrug
Fort Hartley
Dinosaur Footprints
Mosehle
Tosing
Ralebona

Rouxville
R393
Duleriesnek
Quthing
(Moyeni)
Qomoqomong
Quthing
80

Orange River
Sterkspruit
Bluegums
Herschel
Sinxondo
Tele
Ben Macdhui
(3001m)

4

Lundean's Nek
Lundean's Nek
Tiffindell
Naudesnek

Lady Grey
Karringmelkspruit
Avoca Peak
+(2769m)
Witteberge
Pitseng
Elands Height
R58
Rhodes
R396
R393

Kraai River
New England
Mosbesh's Ford
Tsitsana River
121

5

Vineyard
R344
Clanville
Nkulnleko
Barkly East
R392
Tsitsana River
31°S

Jamestown
Clifford
R58
Mooi River
Maclear
108
Washbank Spruit

Swernpoort
Eastern Cape
Barkly Pass
Dyoki
Ugie

6

Rossouw
R344
R396
Barkly
R56
2127m
Bushman Paintings
and Caves
Sinakho
Dordrecht
R56
Morristown
Masibambane
Elliot
Ida
Cala Road
Xalanga
Qiba

E   F   G   H

10   20 km
5   10 mi

Dargle
Midmar Public Resort
Merrivale
Midmar Dam
Hilton
Queen Elizabeth Park
Pietermaritzburg
Ashburton
Edendale
Thornville
Cato Ridge
Camperdown
Mpumalanga
Richmond
Rosebank
Hammarsdale
Kloof
Clermont
Pinetown
Queensburg
KwaMashu
DURBAN
The Bluff

Donnybrook

KwaZulu-Natal

Ndwedwe
Moowood Memorial Gardens
Sheffield Beach
Salt Rock
Shaka's Rock
Tongaat
Ballito Bay
Tongaat
Umdloti
Verulam
Newsel & Umdloti Beach
Inanda
Phoenix
Umhlanga Lagoon Nature Reserve
Umhlanga Rocks

Dolphin Coast

Nagle Dam
Umgeni River

Nshongweni Dam

Ixopo
Umzimkulu
Highflats
Braemar
Vernon Crookes Nature Reserve
Umzinto
Ifala
Ntatabomvu + (822m)

Mkomazi River
Lovu River
Umpambinyoni River
Umtwalume River
Umtwalume

Umlazi
Umbumbulu
Adams Mission
Isipingo
Isipingo
Umbogintwini
Warner Beach
Amanzimtoti
St Winifred's
Winklespruit
Kingsburgh
Karridene
Illovo Beach
Umgababa
Sunlight
Ilfracombe
Umkomaas
Clansthal
Renishaw
Scottburgh
Umzinto North
Park Rynie
Kelso
Pennington
Umdoni Park
Sezela
Ifafa Beach
Mtwalume
Turton
Glen Echo

Durban International

Sunshine Coast

St Faith's
Dweshula
Hibberdene

Umzumbe River
Umzimkulu River

Umzumbe
Pumula
Melville
Anerley
Banana Beach
Bendigo
Southport
Sea Park
Marburg
Umtentweni
Port Shepstone
Oslo Beach
Nqabeni
Izingolweni
Paddock
Izotsha
Shelley Beach
St Michael's-on-Sea
Uvongo
Margate
Redoubt
Ramsgate
Southbroom
San Lameer
Trafalgar
Marina
Palm Beach
Umtamvuna Nature Reserve
Munster
Leisure Crest
Glenmore Beach
Leisure Bay
Port Edward
Banner Rest
Silver
Wild Coast Sun Hotel

Trafalgar Marine Reserve

Hibiscus Coast

INDIAN OCEAN

Impisi
Mnyameni
Umtentu
Msikaba
South Sand Bluff
Port Grosvenor

Hiking Trail

▲ **57** ▲

	A	B	C	D

Konikans

Landplaas

R363

18°E

Kne svlakte

Vanrhynspas

Grootdrif

N7

1

Koekenaap

Lutzville

R362

R363

R27

Vanrhynsdorp

24

Unionskraal

19°E

River

Olifants

30

21

Vredendal

R362

Papendorp

Spruitdrif

23

Klawer

2

Strandfontein

22

Doring Bay

Trawal

58

Heerenlogement

67

Rooiduine Point

Heerenlogement

3

32°S

Ratelfontein

R363

Lambert's Bay

31

R364

31

Graafwater

Clanwilliam

Pak

Wolfhuis

Kliph
State Fo

A T L A N T I C
O C E A N

Leipoldtville

42

Sandberg

Baboon Point

Eland's Bay

14

4

Redelinghuys

28

R363

R366

Paleisheuwel

40

Noordkuil

Het Kruis

Cit

Piekenierskloof

Western Cape

St Helena Bay

Aurora

R366

5

Stompneuspunt

Dwarskersbos

Eendekuil

Stompneusbaai

St Helena
Bay

R399

Pools

R365

Laaiplek

Velddrif

40

Sauer

Goedverwag

25

Cape Columbine

Paternoster

Witwater

Piketberg

Columbine
National Reserve

Vredenburg

Bergrivier

Berg River

De Hoek

6

R44

33°S

Koringberg

Porte

Saldanha

R45

Hopefield

Saldanha Bay

Langebaan

	A	B	C	D

▼ **90** ▼

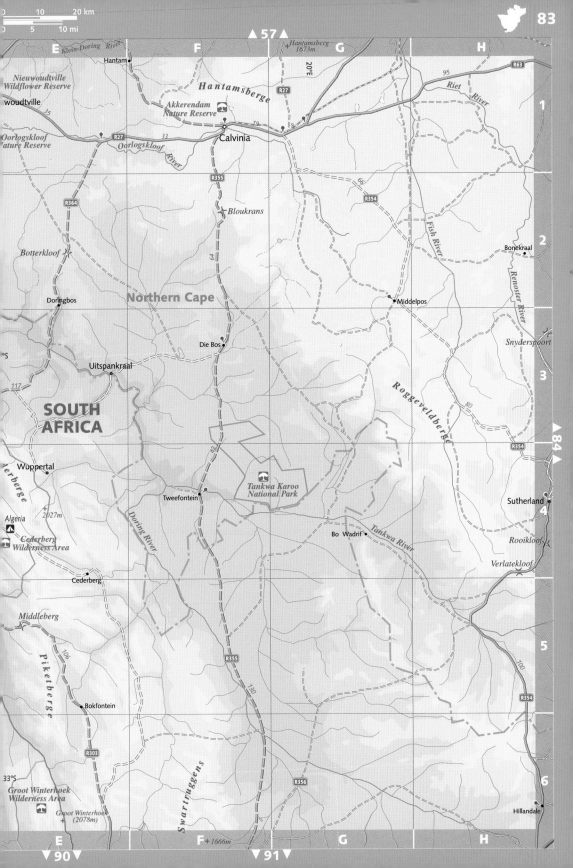

10 20 km
5 10 mi

E   F   G   H

Klein-Doring River

Hantam

Nieuwoudtville Wildflower Reserve

woudtville

35

Akkerendam Nature Reserve

Hantamsberge

Hantamsberg 1673m

20°E

R27

R63

Riet River

95

1

Oorlogskloof
ature Reserve

R27

33

Oorlogskloof River

Calvinia

19

R355

Bloukrans

R354

66

Fish River

Bonekraal

2

R364

69

Botterkloof

Northern Cape

Doringbos

Middelpos

Renoster River

Snyderspoort

°S

Die Bos

Uitspankraal

117

**SOUTH
AFRICA**

Roggeveldberge

80

R354

▲ 84 ▲

3

Wuppertal

erberge

Algeria

2027m

Cederberg
Wilderness Area

42

Tweefontein

Doring River

Tankwa Karoo
National Park

Bo Wadrif

Tankwa River

Sutherland

Rooikloof

Verlatekloof

4

Cederberg

Middleberg

**P
i
k
e
t
b
e
r
g
e**

106

Bokfontein

R355

130

100

R354

5

R303

33°S

*Groot Winterhoek
Wilderness Area*

Groot Winterhoek
(2078m)

**S
w
a
r
t
r
u
g
g
e
n
s**

R356

Hillandale

6

F + 1666m

E   F   G   H

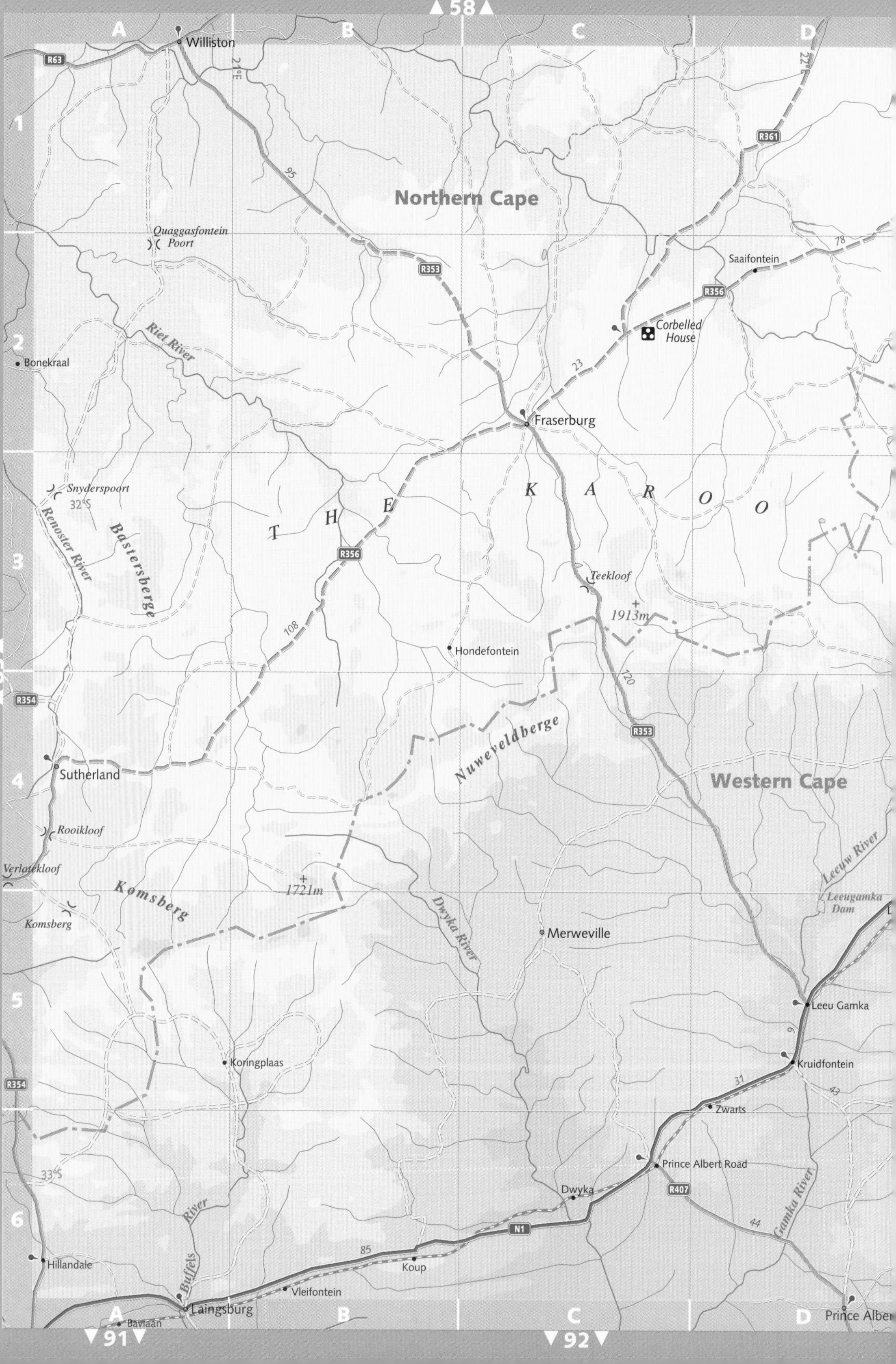

R63

A

Williston

B

▲ 58 ▲

C

D

R361

1

95

Northern Cape

R353

Saaifontein

78

R356

Quaggasfontein
Poort

Corbelled
House

2

23

Bonekraal

Riet River

Fraserburg

Snyderspoort

32°S

Renoster River

Bastersberge

T H E

K A R O O

3

R356

Teekloof

1913m

▲ 83 ▲

108

Hondefontein

720

R354

Nuweveldberge

R353

4

Sutherland

Western Cape

Rooikloof

Verlatekloof

1721m

Komsberg

Dwyka River

Leeuw River

Komsberg

Merweville

Leeugamka
Dam

5

Leeu Gamka

Koringplaas

Kruidfontein

9

R354

31

42

Zwarts

33°S

Prince Albert Road

Buffels River

Gamka River

6

Dwyka

R407

44

Hillandale

N1

85

Koup

A

B

C

D

Prince Albert

Laingsburg

Bavlaan

Vleifontein

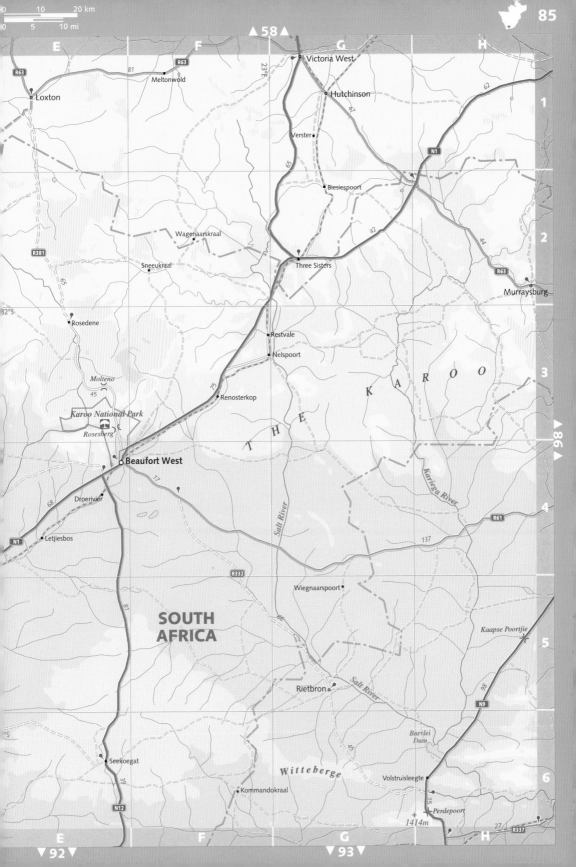

10   20 km
0   5   10 mi

E   F   G   H

R63
Loxton
Meltonwold
R63
81
Victoria West
Hutchinson
62
1
23°E
Verster
N1
65
Biesiespoort
47
2
Wagenaarskraal
42
Three Sisters
44
R63
R381
Sneeukraal
Murraysburg
65
32°S
Rosedene
Restvale
T H E   K A R O O
Nelspoort
3
Molteno
75
Renosterkop
▼ 98 ▼
45
Karoo National Park
Rosesberg
Kariega River
Beaufort West
Salt River
17
4
68
Droerivier
137
R61
N1
Letjiesbos
R332
Kaapse Poortjie
81
SOUTH
AFRICA
Wiegnaarspoort
5
66
N9
Rietbron
Salt River
Barvlei
Dam
45
81
Witteberge
Volstruisleegte
6
Seekoegat
15
Perdepoort
39
Kommandokraal
1414m
27
R337
N12
98

E   F   G   H

▲ 59 ▲

A | B | C | D

Richmond

Onders River

24°E

R398

Northern Cape

R56

25°E

Middelburg

Rosmead

1

109

Heydon

N9

Tafelbe

35

Witkransnek

Cor

Sneeuberg

+ 2504m

55

Lootsberg

24

R388

2

Nieu-Bethesda

Bethesdaweg

× *Wapadsberg*

Spitskopvlei

30

R61

Murraysburg

32

48

Naudesberg

Agter Sneeuberg

32°S

R63

60

Valley of Desolation

Western Cape

Ouberg

Bankberg

3

Petersburg

Van
Ryneveld's
Pass Dam

Graaff-Reinet

Karoo

▲ 85 ▲

Nature Reserve

+ 2013

Munnikspoort

Adendorp

Barakke

54

Behulpsaam

T H E

Behulpsaam

4

R61

Aberdeen

K A R O O

R63

58

34

R337

N9

Kendrew

Pearston

R338

40

Sundays River

65

R337

Bruintjieshoo

R75

Vogel River

Aberdeen Road

56

5

Vogel River

Oatlands

Eastern Cape

R75

33°S

C Soutpansnek

12

Klipplaat

Jansenville

35

49

Miller

+ 1450m

33

Waterford

Swanepoelspoort

R338

6

Grootrivierhoogte

Mount Stewart

Greystone

*Darlington
Dam*

R337

Groot River

R329

Baroe

A | B | C | D

0 10 20 km
0 5 10 mi

E　　　F　　　G　　　H

Schoombee
Syfergat
Penhoek 2127m
White Kei River

R391
Boesmanshoek
Bamboesberg
Sterkstroom

Groatvlak River
R390
Hofmeyr
Eastern Cape
R392

Teviot
R401
R390
R344
Bailey
Qoqodala

Grassridge Dam
R390
Bongolo Dam

Visrivier
Swart Kei River
Bowker's Park
Queenstown
Ezibeleni

Baroda
R61
Tarkastad
R61
R67

Chalmers
N10
Kamastone
Tsolwana Game Reserve
Hukuwa
Whittlesea

Cradock
Elandsdrif
Sada
Guildford

Mountain Zebra National Park
Lake Arthur
Spring Valley
R351
R67
Waterdown Dam

Halesowen
Winterberge
Fairford

Swaershoekpas
Mortimer
Devils Bellows Nek
Katberge

Drennan
Cameron's Glen
Katberg
Balfour

Swaershoek
Glenrock
R344
Katberg
Seymour

Witmos
Daggaboersnek
Liddleton
Hogsback

Bosberg Nature Reserve
Daggaboersnek
Mpofu Game Reserve
Amherst
Upper Tyume
Pleasant View

East Poort
Bedford
Adelaide
Tidbury's Toll

Somerset East
R63
Blinkwater
Fort Beaufort
Fort Hare

Cookhouse
Alice
Middeldrift

Golden Valley
R350
Long Hope
R67

Middleton
Fort Willshire

Little Fish River
Sheldon
Double Drift Game Reserve
Lekfontein

Klipfontein
R335
Carlisle Bridge
R344
Fish River
Breakfast Vlei

N10
R350
Fort Brown
Great Fish River Reserve

R400
Riebeek Oos
Ecca
Committees

Zuurberg
Ann's Villa
Fort Selwyn
N2

▲ 79 ▲

SOUTH AFRICA

Eastern Cape

R392

White Kei River

Indwe
Braunville
Qoqodala
Cacadu
Lady Frere
R396
Driver's Drift
Xonxa Dam
Ida
Xalanga
Garryowen
Askeaton
R393
Cala Road
Qiba
Cala
Calapas
Lufuta
Southeyville
Lubisi Dam
Ncora Dam
Satansnek
Engcobo
All Saints Nek
Tsazo
Langdon
Coghlan
Ku-Mayima
Whitmor
Clarkebury
Bashee E

Bongolo Dam
Queenstown
Ezibeleni
Bolotwa
Qamata
R61
Cofimvaba
St Marks
Qombolo
Hange
Tsomo
Garner's Drift
Ncora
Nobokwe
Munyu
Colleywob
Idutywa
Ebenc
Taler

Swart Kei River
Tylden
Guildford
Waqu
Cathcart
Fairford
R345
Belgrove
Bacela
R351
R352
Xolobe
Nqamaqwe
Ntseshe
Butterworth
Lora River

N6
Toise River
Bolo Reserve
Mgwali
New Nek
Great Kei River
Kei Cuttings
Qoboqobo
Kentani
Kobonqaba
Catspas

Kologha Forest Reserve
Dohne
Bethel
Ross
Grays
Prospect
R63
Komga
N2
Mpetu
R349
Kei Mouth
Gxara
Quko
Kei Mouth
Kei Me
Morgan's Bay

Hogsback
Upper Tyume
Pleasant View
Stutterheim
Gaika's Grave
Amabele
Kei Road
Macleantown
Tainton
Cape Henderson Nature Reserve
Cintsa
Haga-Haga

Keiskammahoek
Amatola Mountains
Maden Dam
R352
Braunschweig
R346
Nahoon River
Mpongo Park
Gonubie River
Cintsa Bay

Middeldrift
R400
Dimbaza
R346
Bisho
Berlin
Kwara River

King William's Town
Kwa-Pita
Breidbach
Zwelitsha
Laing Dam
Potsdam
Dawn
Beacon Bay
Gonubie
Bonza Bay
Nahoon Reef

Fort Willshire
Lekfontein
Sittingbourne
Fort Murray
Mdantsane
East London

Great Fish River Reserve
Breakfast Vlei
R345
N2
Keiskamma River
Tyata
Punzana
R347
Chalumna
Kidd's Beach

Peddie
Wooldridge
R72
Bell
R345
Hamburg
Kiwane Resort

N2

▼ 95 ▼
▲ 87 ▲

10   20 km

0   5

10 mi

E

F

G

H

Sidwadweni

Stoneyridge

Luchaba
Nature Reserve
Nobantu

Umtata Dam

Rock of Execution

Libode

Mlenganapas

Lusikisiki

South Sand Bluff
Port Grosvenor

Umtafulu River

Umzimpunzi

Mbotyi

Mgoma
Monteku

R61

Misty Mount

Mngazana River

95

Ntambalala
Agate Terrace

Umtata

Buntingville

Nduli
Nature Reserve

Ngqeleni

Old Bunting

Ntshilini

Gemvale

Tombo

Mnganzana Mouth

Port St Johns

Silaka

Silaka
Nature Reserve

Viedgesville

Mdumbi River

Notintsila

Mpande
The Kraal

Qunu

Mqanduli

Ngqungqu

Umtata River

50

Old Morley

Tshani

*Hluleka
Nature Reserve*

Hluleka

Ngciba

Walking
Trail

W i l d   C o a s t

32°S

ptdale (Xhora)

Coffee Bay

Hole in the Wall;
Ocean View Hotel

Mbashe River

Mhlahlane

Mpame   *Mnewasa Point*

Amanzimyama

Alderley

Xora River

Rothmere

Xora

Nqabara River

Wild

Coast

Hobeni

Cwebe
Nature Reserve
The Haven

Ciko

llowvale

Mbashe

Dwesa
Nature Reserve

yokana

Nqabara

Dwesa

Shixini

Manubi

Qora Mouth

Mazeppa Point

Cebe

avecrest

I N D I A N   O C E A N

33°S

E

F

G

H

R61

29°E

30°E

▲ 82 ▲   ▲ 83 ▲

ATLANTIC OCEAN

Hopefield

Langebaan

Posberg
National
Reserve

Churchhaven

Langebaan
Lagoon

West Coast
National Park

Yzerfontein

Dassen
Island

The Grotto Bay

Bok Point
Bok Bay

Atlantis

Moorreesburg

Rust

Malmesbury

Abbotsdale

Kalbaskraal

Philadelphia

Melkbosstrand

Robben Island

Table Bay

Bloubergstrand

Milnerton

Parow

Durbanville

Kraaifontein

Bellville

CAPE TOWN

Clifton Beach

Camp's Bay

Table Mountain
(1073m)

Cape Town
International

Kirstenbosch
Botanic Gardens

Llandudno

Hout Bay

Hout Bay

Noordhoek

Chapman's Bay

Kommetjie

Witsands

Kalk Bay

Muizenberg

Fish Hoek

Simon's Bay

Simon's Town

Olifantsbospunt

Cape of Good Hope
Nature Reserve

Cape of Good Hope

Cape Point

Partridge Point

Buffels Bay

Nyanga

Mitchells Plain

Khayelitsha

Faure

Firgrove

Kuilsrivier

Somerset West

Strand

Gordon's Bay

Sir Lowry's

Grabouw

Elgin

Vredendal

Botrivier

Houhoek

False Bay

Kogel Bay

Buffelstalberg
(884m)

Rooiels Bay

Pringle Bay

Kleinmond

Babilonstoring
(1169m)

Hangklip

Betty's Bay

Pringle Bay

Cape Hangklip

Sanddown Bay

Hawston

Onrus

Hermanus

Stanfo

Walker Bay

Gansbaai

Danger Point

Sandy

Darling

Tienie Versveld
Flower Reserve

Modder River

Mamre

Riebeek Wes

Riebeek Kasteel

Bothmaskloof

Hermon

Bailey's Peak
(1519m)

Wellington

Mbekweni

Windmill

Paarl

Paarl Mountain
Nature Reserve

Klein
Drakenstein

Huguenot
Toll Tunnel

Boschendal

Pniel

Helshoogte

Stellenbosch

Hottentots Holland
Nature Reserve

Franschhoek

Franschhoek

Aasvoëlberg
(1644m)

Villiersdorp

Theewaterskloof
Dam

Wemmershoek
Dam

Wemmershoekberge

Franschhoekberge

Du Toitskloof

Rawsonville

Worceste

Gouda

Tulbagh

Prince Alfred
Hamlet

Ceres

Ceres Nature Reser

Wolseley

Michell's
Buffelshoekpiek
(2062m)

Sybasberg
(1902m)

Hexrivierber

Karoo Nati
Botanic Gar

Bainskloof

Groot Winterhoek
Wilderness Area

Groot Winterhoek
(2078m)

Saronberg
(1800m)

Gydopas

Nuwekloofpas

Voëlvlei
Dam

Lanet River

Dutoitspiek
(1997m)

Greater
Brandvlei
Dam

Moor

Hamma

Caledor

K

Kleinmond

▲ 83 ▲   ▲ 84 ▲

E   F   G   H

10   20 km
5   10 mi

+ 1666m
R356
Die Venster
Hottentotskloof
SOUTH
AFRICA
Matroosberg
(2251m)
Verkeerdevlei
Touws River
Zuurplaats
(1382m)
Pieter Meintjies
64
Matjiesfontein
Baviaan
Laingsburg
Vleifontein
Kragershoek
(1344m)
Witteberge
Paradehoek
(1474m)
Rooinek
Floriskraal
Dam
1

Hex River
N1
75
Tunnel
Matroosberg
Avondrust
Bloutoring
Touws River
Anys River
Anysberg
(1623m)
Prinsrivier-
Dam
Anysberg
Prins River
R323
Rouxpos
Groot River
De Doorns
Kwadousberg
Karoo River
80
Nouga Hills
Patatsfontein
(1387m)
Little Karoo
Waboomsberg
(1428m)
Ouberg
Langkloof
Boerboonfontein
Bellair
Dam
Warmwaterberg
Brak River
65
Plathuis
Warmwaterberg
2

+ eromsberg
(2075m)
Keeromdam
R318
Keisie River
Dassieshoek
(1700m)
Waboomsberg
Burgers
Kleinberg
(1115m)
Kalkoenshoek River
Jakalsfontein
(1352m)
Lemoenshoek
Nuy
R60
50
Mineral Baths
Montagu
Robertson
Kogmanskloof
Ashton
R62
Langeberge
Groot River
48
63
Barrydale
R324
Zuurbrak
(1508m)
Tradouw
(1364m)
Brandrivier
3

Breede River
Vrolijkheid
Nature Reserve
Bonnievale
Marloth
Nature Reserve
Zuurbrak
Tradouw
34°S
McGregor
Poesjenels River
Groot River
70
Swellendam
13
15
Suurbraak
30

kop
46m)
adendal
Greyton
Skilpadskop
(1510m)
Pilaarkop
(1655m)
Stormsvlei
25
Bontebok
National Park
Heidelberg
N2
Askraal
92 ▲
4

wartberg
1089m)
R406
Dwarskloof
Lindeshof
N2
8
23
Riviersonderend
Western Cape
R324
R322
Slang River
33
Rietpoel
R317
Klipdale
Protem
60
Malgas
Vermaaklikheid
Oukraal
R326
R316
Salt River
Ouplas
Wydgeleë
Breede River
Potberg
(612m)
Port Beaufort
Whitesands
5

ersberg
Tafelberg
(845m)
Akkedisbergpas
28
46
Fairfield
Bredasdorpberge
Napier
Noormanskop
(624m)
R319
De Hoop
Vlei
De Hoop
Nature Reserve
Elandspad
Infanta-on-River
St Sebastian Bay
Cape Infanta
Salmonsdam
Nature Reserve
Papiesvlei
Bredasdorp
Skipskop
Elim
25
Baardskeerdersbos
R319
R316
Marcus Bay
Viljoenshof
Pearly Beach
R317
Waenhuiskrans (Arniston)
Struis Point
INDIAN
OCEAN

Soetendalsvlei
Struis Bay
Quoin Point
Die Dam
Hotagterklip
Struisbaai
L'Agulhas
Cape Agulhas
6

E   F   G   H

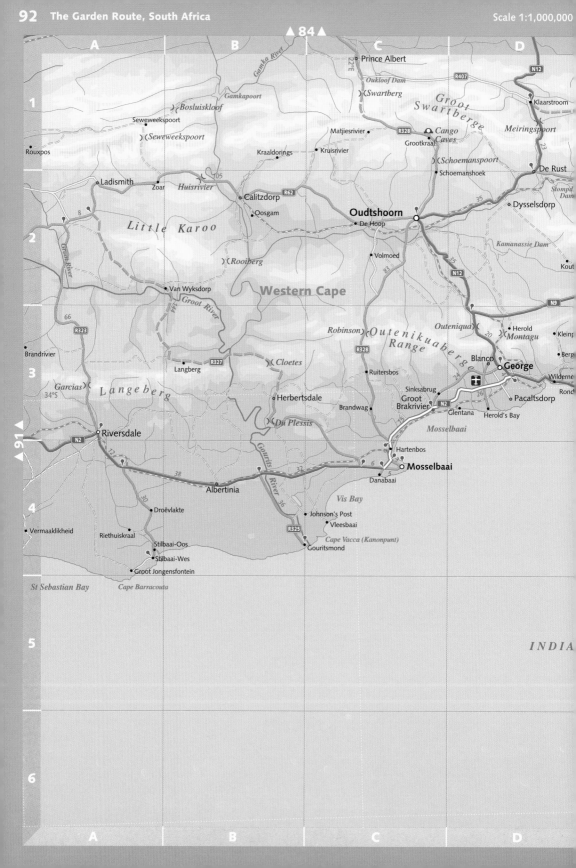

▲ 84 ▲

A B C D

1

Rouxpos

Bosluiskloof

Seweekspoort

Gamkapoort

Gamka River

Prince Albert

Oukloof Dam

Swartberg

Groot Swartberge

R407

Klaarstroom

N12

Meiringspoort

23

Seweekspoort

Kraaldorings

Kruisrivier

Matjiesrivier

R328

Cango Caves

Grootkraal

Schoemanspoort

Schoemanshoek

De Rust

Stompd Dam

2

Ladismith

Zoar

Huisrivier

105

Calitzdorp

R62

Oosgam

Little Karoo

Rooiberg

De Hoop

Oudtshoorn

Volmoed

35

83

35

N12

Dysselsdorp

Kamanassie Dam

Kout

8

Grain River

Van Wyksdorp

Groot River

Western Cape

66

R323

Brandrivier

Robinson

R328

Outeniqua

Range

Outeniquaberge

20

Herold

Montagu

Kleinp

Berg

3

Garcias

34°S

Langberg

Langeberg

R327

Cloetes

Herbertsdale

Brandwag

Ruitersbos

Sinksabrug

Groot Brakrivier

N2

24

26

Blanco

George

Wildern

Rond

Pacaltsdorp

Glentana

Herold's Bay

Herold's Bay

91

N2

Riversdale

Du Plessis

Gouritz River

Mosselbaai

4

Droëvlakte

Albertinia

Vermaaklikheid

Riethuiskraal

Stilbaai-Oos

Stilbaai-Wes

Groot Jongensfontein

12

30

38

32

36

Hartenbos

Danabaai

6

5

Mosselbaai

Vis Bay

Johnson's Post

Vleesbaai

R325

Cape Vacca (Kanonpunt)

Gouritsmond

St Sebastian Bay

Cape Barracouta

5

INDIA

6

A B C D

0 10 20 km
0 5 10 mi

E   F   G   H

▲ 85 ▲
Perdepoort
1414m

30

R329

Willowmore

Buyspoort

Ghwarriepoort 34

Baviaanskloofberge

165

Studtis

R332

Sandvlakte

Colekeplaas

Nuwekluf

R407 95

Fanis River

R341

R339

N9

12

20

22

Zaaimansdal

SOUTH
AFRICA

Kougaberge

Eastern Cape

1

2

Buffelsdrif

Potjiesberg   Uniondale

mmanassieberge

Uniondale
Poort

Avontuur

11

Haarlem

Misgund

R62

Louterwater

Joubertina

171

Kammiebos

Assegaaibos

Kareedouw

Daskop Molenrivier 71 Speelmans Kraal

Noll

36

De Vlug

Keurbooms River

Prince Alfred's

Tsitsikammaberge

1715m

Kouga River

Barrington   Homtini

R339

35

The Crags   Grootrivier   De Vasselot
Rustcamp

Bloukrans

Paul Sauer
Bridge

Tsitsikamma

13

6

R340

Keurbooms
Nature Reserve

21

Stormsrivier

34°S

Woodlands

3

Wilderness
National Park

Phantom

Knysna National
Lake Area

N2

Wittedrift

Nature's Valley

Tsitsikamma Coastal
National Park

Storms River Mouth

63

Goukamma
Nature Reserve

36

Sedgefield Buffalo
Bay

Knysna

The
Heads

Noetzie

Plettenberg Bay

Walker Point Brenton-
on-Sea

Cape Seal

Robberg Nature
& Marine Reserve

▲ 94 ▲

4

CEAN

5

6

E   F   G   H

24°E   60

23°E

▲ 86 ▲

A **B** **C** **D**

Ann's Villa

Baroe

Darlington Dam

Zuurberg

29

26

Wolwefontein

Kleinpoort

25°E

Vogel River

Zuurberg National Park

Suurberg

1

Steytlerville

50

Glenconnor

24

Kirkwood

19

Coerney

Sunland

38

Bluecliff

15

Lendlovu

Addo Eleph National Pa

SOUTH AFRICA

R75

Addo

33

Colekeplaas

Grootwinterhoekberge

Smitskraal

Cambria

Cockscomb 1759m

Swartkops River

Melkhoutboom

Tip Tree

Groendal Dam

Kinkelt

R335

Colc

2

Kouga Dam

Demistkraal

37

Patensie

Gamtos River

R331

Andrieskraal

Hankey

26

Eastern Cape

8

Uitenhage

22

14

30

N2

Coega

Algoa Be

R332

21

Loerie

Despatch

17

R368

R334

Amsterdamhoek

Swartkops

Hobie Beach

Bethelsdorp

16

20

Assegaaibos

35

Van Stadens Wild Flower Reserve

Thornhill

18

14

Walmer

11

Fort Frederick

Summerstrand

Kareedouw

34°S

Witteklip

PORT ELIZABETH

16

3

Clarkson

77

N2

16

Kruisfontein

35

17

Sea View

38

Skoenmakerskop

Cape Recife

Humansdorp

24

Jeffreys Bay

Jeffreys Bay

R330

Aston Bay

St Francis Bay

Paradysstrand

Slangrivier

St Francis Bay

Oyster Bay

Tsitsikamma Point

Cape St Francis

Cape St Francis

Cape St Francis

▲ 93 ▲

4

5

6

A **B** **C** **D**

10   20 km
5   10 mi

E   F   G   H

lifantskop Alicedale
Bellevue
Shamwari
Game Reserve

Fort Selwyn
Grahamstown

Peddie
Wooldridge
Bell
Hamburg

R345   16

65
N2

26°E

Wesley
Bira River
Keiskama Point   1

Round Hill
Nature Reserve

Fallodon   37

Kariega River

sa
terson

Langholm

Kowie River

55

Great Fish River

Mpekweni Sun

44
Salem
Bathurst
Fish River Sun

75

Bushmans River
43
Southwell
R67   30
Great Fish Point

16
2
16

Ncanaha   22

R72   54

R343   R72

23

Great Fish Point

Alexandria
Kariega
Kasouga
Port Alfred
Port Alfred

Kenton-on-Sea
Bushman's River Mouth
Boknesstrand
(Richmond)

oringmount   Cornville

Shipwreck Coast

Cape Padrone

34°S   3

4

INDIAN OCEAN   5

6

E   F   G   H

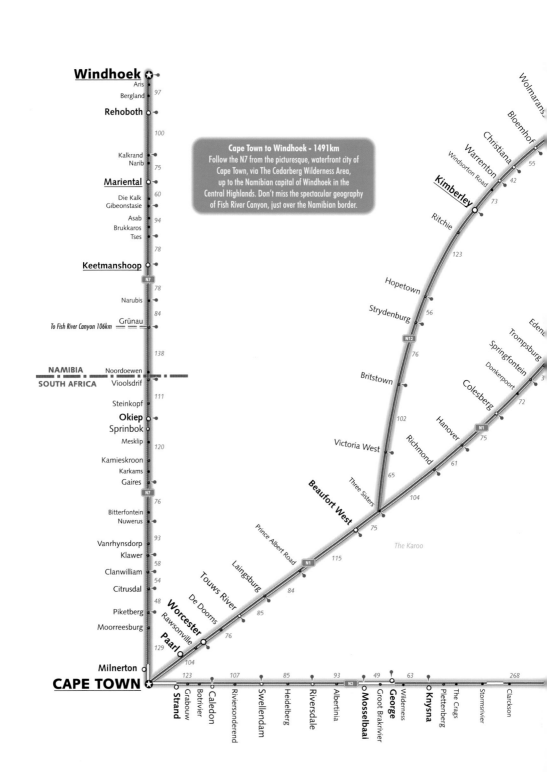

Windhoek
Aris
Bergland • 97
Rehoboth
100
Kalkrand
Narib • 75
Mariental
Die Kalk 60
Gibeonstasie
Asab 94
Brukkaros
Tses 78
Keetmanshoop
N7
78
Narubis
84
Grünau
To Fish River Canyon 106km
138
NAMIBIA — Noordoewen
SOUTH AFRICA — Viooolsdrif 111
Steinkopf
Okiep
Sprinbok
Mesklip 120
Kamieskroon
Karkams
Gaires
N7
76
Bitterfontein
Nuwerus
93
Vanrhynsdorp
Klawer 58
Clanwilliam 54
Citrusdal 48
Piketberg
Moorreesburg
Worcester De Doorns
Paarl Rawsonville
129
Milnerton 104
CAPE TOWN 123

Cape Town to Windhoek - 1491km
Follow the N7 from the picturesque, waterfront city of
Cape Town, via The Cedarberg Wilderness Area,
up to the Namibian capital of Windhoek in the
Central Highlands. Don't miss the spectacular geography
of Fish River Canyon, just over the Namibian border.

Wolmarans
Bloemhof
Christiana 55
Warrenton 42
Windsorton Road
Kimberley 73
Ritchie
123
Hopetown
Strydenburg 56
N12
76
Britstown
Colesberg
Springfontein
Donkerpoort
Eden
Trompsburg
3
72
Hanover
N1
75
Victoria West Richmond 61
65
Beaufort West Three Sisters
104
75
The Karoo
Prince Albert Road
N1 115
Laingsburg
Touws River 84
85
76

Strand
Grabouw
Botrivier
Caledon
Riviersonderend
Swellendam
Heidelberg
Riversdale
Albertinia
Mosselbaai
Groot Brakrivier
George
Wilderness
Knysna
Plettenberg
The Crags
Stormsrivier
Clarckson
123
107
85
93 N2 49
63
268

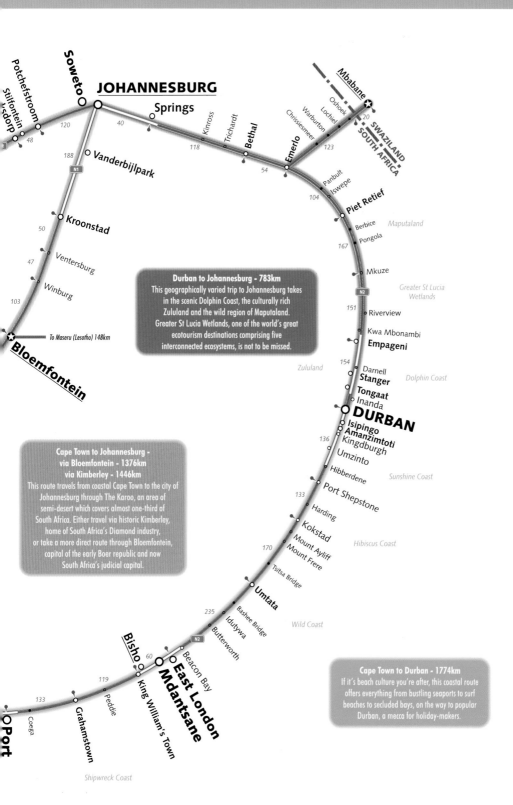

Soweto

Potchefstroom
Stilfontein
sdorp

JOHANNESBURG

Springs

120   40

48

188   N1   Vanderbijlpark

Kinross
Trichardt
Bethal

118

Chrissiesmeer

Emerlo

Warburton
Lochiel
Oshoek

Mbabane

⭐

20

SWAZILAND
SOUTH AFRICA

123

54

Panbult
Iswepe

104   **Piet Retief**

50   **Kroonstad**

Berbice   *Maputaland*

167   Pongola

47   Ventersburg

Winburg

103

⭐

Bloemfontein

To Maseru (Lesotho) 148km

Durban to Johannesburg - 783km
This geographically varied trip to Johannesburg takes
in the scenic Dolphin Coast, the culturally rich
Zululand and the wild region of Maputaland.
Greater St Lucia Wetlands, one of the world's great
ecotourism destinations comprising five
interconnected ecosystems, is not to be missed.

Mkuze

N2

*Greater St Lucia
Wetlands*

151   Riverview

Kwa Mbonambi

Empageni

154

Darnell
Stanger

Tongaat
Inanda

Dolphin Coast

Zululand

DURBAN

**Cape Town to Johannesburg -
via Bloemfontein - 1376km
via Kimberley - 1446km**
This route travels from coastal Cape Town to the city of
Johannesburg through The Karoo, an area of
semi-desert which covers almost one-third of
South Africa. Either travel via historic Kimberley,
home of South Africa's Diamond industry,
or take a more direct route through Bloemfontein,
capital of the early Boer republic and now
South Africa's judicial capital.

Isipingo
Amanzimtoti
136   Kingdburgh

Umzinto

Hibberdene

Sunshine Coast

133   Port Shepstone

Harding

Kokstad

170   Mount Ayliff
Mount Frere

Hibiscus Coast

Tsitsa Bridge

Umtata

235   Bashee Bridge
Idutywa

Butterworth

Wild Coast

Bisho   60   Beacon Bay

N2

East London
Mdantsane

119   King William's Town

133   Peddie

Coega   Grahamstown

Port

Shipwreck Coast

Cape Town to Durban - 1774km
If it's beach culture you're after, this coastal route
offers everything from bustling seaports to surf
beaches to secluded bays, on the way to popular
Durban, a mecca for holiday-makers.

Not drawn to scale

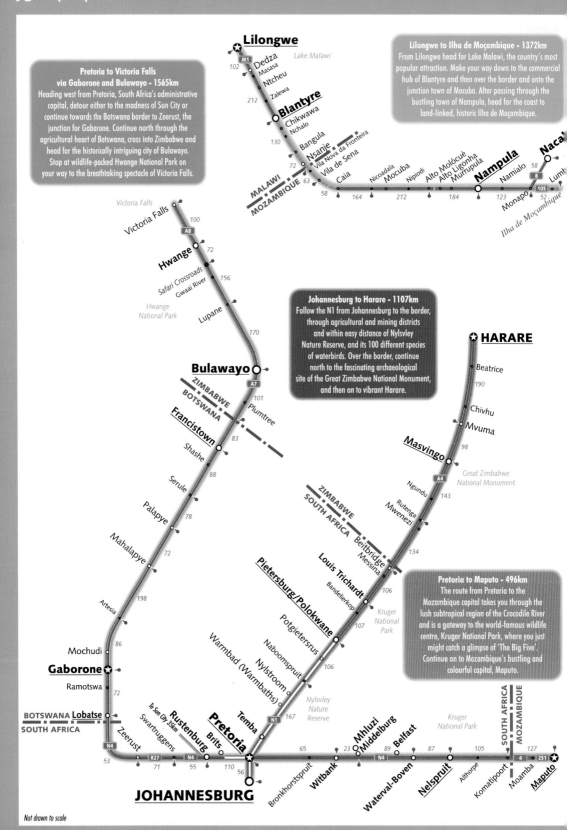

Lilongwe
M1
102
Dedza
Masasa
Ntcheu
Zalewa

Lake Malawi

212

Blantyre
Chikwawa
Nchalo
130
Bangula
Nsanje
72
Vila Nova da Fronteira
Vila de Sena
63
Caia
58
164
Nicoadala
212
Mocuba
Nipiodi
184
Alto Molócuè
Alto Ligonha
Murrupula
123
Nampula
Narnialo
58
8
105
52
Monapo
Lumb
Naca

Ilha de Moçambique

MALAWI
MOZAMBIQUE

Lilongwe to Ilha de Moçambique - 1372km
From Lilongwe head for Lake Malawi, the country's most popular attraction. Make your way down to the commercial hub of Blantyre and then over the border and onto the junction town of Mocuba. After passing through the bustling town of Nampula, head for the coast to land-linked, historic Ilha de Moçambique.

**Pretoria to Victoria Falls
via Gaborone and Bulawayo - 1565km**
Heading west from Pretoria, South Africa's administrative capital, detour either to the madness of Sun City or continue towards the Botswana border to Zeerust, the junction for Gaborone. Continue north through the agricultural heart of Botswana, cross into Zimbabwe and head for the historically intriguing city of Bulawayo. Stop at wildlife-packed Hwange National Park on your way to the breathtaking spectacle of Victoria Falls.

Victoria Falls
Victoria Falls
100
A8
72
Hwange
Safari Crossroads
156
Gwaai River
*Hwange
National Park*
Lupane
170

Johannesburg to Harare - 1107km
Follow the N1 from Johannesburg to the border, through agricultural and mining districts and within easy distance of Nylsvley Nature Reserve, and its 100 different species of waterbirds. Over the border, continue north to the fascinating archaeological site of the Great Zimbabwe National Monument, and then on to vibrant Harare.

Bulawayo
A7
101
Plumtree
ZIMBABWE
BOTSWANA
Francistown
83
Shashe
88
Serule
Palapye
78
Mahalapye
72
Artesia
198
Mochudi
86
Gaborone
Ramotswa
72

HARARE
Beatrice
190
Chivhu
Mvuma
Masvingo
98
A4
*Great Zimbabwe
National Monument*
Ngundu
143
Rutenga
Mwenezi
ZIMBABWE
SOUTH AFRICA
Beitbridge
Messina
134

Louis Trichardt
Bandelierkop
106
*Kruger
National
Park*
107

Pietersburg/Polokwane
Potgietersrus
Naboomspruit
Nylstroom
106
Warmbad (Warmbaths)
*Nylsvley
Nature
Reserve*

Pretoria to Maputo - 496km
The route from Pretoria to the Mozambique capital takes you through the lush subtropical region of the Crocodile River and is a gateway to the world-famous wildlife centre, Kruger National Park, where you just might catch a glimpse of 'The Big Five'. Continue on to Mozambique's bustling and colourful capital, Maputo.

BOTSWANA **Lobatse**
SOUTH AFRICA
Zeerust
N4
53
R27
71
N4
55
110
56

To Sun City 35km
Swartruggens
Rustenburg
Brits
Pretoria
Temba
N1
167

JOHANNESBURG

Bronkhorstspruit
65
Witbank
23
Mhluzi
Middelburg
89
Belfast
87
Waterval-Boven
Nelspruit
Althorpe
105
Komatipoort
Moamba
127
Maputo
N4
4
251
SOUTH AFRICA
MOZAMBIQUE
*Kruger
National
Park*

Not drawn to scale

ROUTES

Freeway
Autoroute
Autobahn
Autovía

Primary Road
Route Principale
Fernstraße
Carretera Principal

Secondary Road
Route Secondaire
Nebenstraße
Carretera Secundaria

Street; Lane
Rue; Allée
Straße; Gasse
Calle; Paseo

On/Off Ramp
Entrées/sorties d' autoroute
Straßenauf
Entrada/Salida

Unsealed Roads
Route non bitumée
unversiegelte Straße
Carretera sin Asfaltar

Pedestrian Mall
Zone construite
Fußgängerzone
Zona Peatonal

Path
Sentier pédestre
Pfad
Sendero

Footbridge
Passerelle
Fußgängerbrücke
Puente Peatonal

One Way Street
Sens unique
Einbahnstraße
Calle de Sentido Único

TRANSPORTATION

Railway
Voie de chemin de fer
Eisenbahn
Ferrocarril

Ferry; Ferry Terminal
Route de ferry; Terminal du ferry
Fährroute; Fähranlegestelle
Transbordador; Estación Marítima

MISCELLANEOUS

Ancient Wall
Ancien mur d'enceinte
altertümliche Stadtmauer
Muro Antiguo

AREA FEATURES

Major Building
Bâtiment
Hauptgebäude
Edificio Importante

Hotel
Hôtel
Hotel
Hotel

Shops; Market
Magasins; Marché
Geschäfte; Markt
Tiendas; Mercado

Park
Parc
Park
Parque

Theatre
Théâtre
Theater
Teatro

Cemetery; Campus
Cimetière; Campus
Friedhof; Campus
Cementerio; Campus

SYMBOLS

Bus Station
Station de bus
Bushaltestelle
Estación de Autobuses

Church
Église
Kirche
Iglesia

Embassy, Consulate
Ambassade, Consulat
Botschaft, Konsulat
Embajada, Consulado

Golf Course
Terrain de Golf
Golfplatz
Campo de Golf

Hospital
Hôpital
Krankenhaus
Hospital

Internet Café
Café Internet
Internet Café
Servicio local de Internet

Mosque
Mosquée
Moschee
Mezquita

Parking Area
Parking
Parkplatz
Aparcamiento

Point of Interest
Curiosités
Sehenswerter Ort
Punto de Interés

Pool
Piscine
Schwimmbad
Piscina

Telephone
Téléphone
Telefon
Teléfono

Camping Ground
Terrain de Camping
Zeltplatz
Camping

Cinema
Cinéma
Kino
Cine

Gardens
Jardins
Gärten
Jardines

Hindu Temple
Temple Hindouiste
Hindu Tempel
Templo Hindú

Information Centre
Centre d'information
Informationszentrum
Centro de Información

Monument
Monument
Denkmal
Monumento

Museum
Musée
Museum
Museo

Petrol Station
Station-Service
Tankstelle
Gasolinera

Police Station
Police
Polizeirevier
Comisaría

Post Office
Bureau de Poste
Postamt
Correos y Telégrafos

Zoo
Jardine Zoologique
Zoo
Parque Zoológico

A | B | C | D

Elbow

East Pier

Duncan Dock

B Berth

C Berth

D Berth

E Berth

F Berth

G Berth

Foreshore

Duncan Rd

To Paarl

Table Bay Blvd

Coen St

South Arm

South Arm

Collier Jetty

Cross Berth

Quay 7

No 2 Jetty

Victoria Basin

Coodes St

Dock Rd

Alfred St

Quay 6

Table Bay

Fish Quay

Fish Market Rd

West Quay

Port Rd

Western Blvd

Hospital St

Alfred St

M6

Quay 5

No 1 Jetty (Robben Island Tours)

Agfa Amphitheatre

Bertie's Landing

Penny Ferry

Old Clock Tower

East Quay

West Quay

Ebenezer Rd

Cardiff St

Bennett St

Battery St

Prestwich St

Alfred St

Victoria Wharf

Market Square

Quay 4

Old Port Captain's Building

Victoria & Alfred

Alfred Basin

Cape Grace

Napier St

Information

Red Shed Craft Workshop

IMAX

Union Castle Building

NSRI

Museum Ships

Small Vessel Marina

Somerset St

De Smidt St

Highfield St

East Pier Road

BMW Pavilion

New Somerset St

Victoria & Alfred Waterfront

Dock Road

South African Maritime Museum

Aquarium

Common Dock

Dock Rd

Gallows Hill Rd

The Waterkant

Portswood Square

Portswood Rd

Waterkant

Loader St

Grange St

Beach Rd

Graduate School of Business

Dock Rd

Foreshore

Strand St

Fort Wynyard Rd

City

Fort Wynyard Museum

Green Point Track

Western Blvd

Main Dve

Hillside Tce

Boundary Rd

Old Muslim Cemetery

Metropolitan Golf Course

Braemar Rd

Wessels Rd

Vesperdene Rd

Upper Portswood Rd

Cavalcade

Chepstow Rd

Carreg Cres

Noon Gun

Fritz Sonnenberg Rd

Bill Peters Dve

Green Point Stadium

Western Blvd

Main Dve

Green Point

Varneys Rd

York Rd

Thornhill Rd

High Level Rd

Ocean View Dve

Merriman Rd

To Signal Hill

Vlei Rd

Green Point Common

To Sea Point & Camps Bay

M5

M51

Dysart Rd

Wigtown Rd

To Sea Point

A | B | C | D

125   250 m
125   250 yd

E   F   G   H

1

D F Malan St
Nico Malan
Bartolemeu Dias St
Salazar St
Vasco da Gama St
Hertzog Blvd
Civic Ave
Civic Centre
Old Marine Dve
Strand St
Pirow St
Oswald
To Cape Town International Airport & Stellenbosch
M50
K102
Sir Lowry Rd
Sidney St
Gore St
Balen St
Sorey La
Tennant St
M6
Cape Technikon
District Six (Zonnebloem)

2

Roggebaai Square
Connection Internet Café
Jetty St
Lower Long
Heerengracht
Tulbagh Square
Jan & Maria van Riebeeck Statues
Pier Place
British Airways Travel Clinic
American Express
Thibault Square
Hans Strijdom St
Merriman Square
Cape Town Train Station
Adderley St
Namibia Trade & Wet House
City Bus Terminal
Minibus Taxi Ranks
Castle St
Fruit & Vegetable Market
Flower Sellers
Bus Information Kiosk
Grand Parade
Buitenkant St
Darling St
Town Hall
Castle of Good Hope
P
Magistrates Court
M39
Caledon St
Harrington St
District Six Museum
Canterbury St
Bloemhof St
Keizersgracht
De Korte St
Werf St
Hanover St
Constitution St
Mount Rd
Primrose St
Drury La
Caledon St
To Newlands, Muizenburg & Simon's Town

3

Mechau St
Prestwich St
Bree St
Riebeek St
Long St
Loop St
Koopmans de Wet House
Lower Burg
Waterkant St
St George's St Mall
Golden Acre Centre
Woolworths
Post Net
OK Bazaars
GPO
Lower Plein St
Pharmacy
Trafalgar Pl
Cape Town Tourism
Sendinmestig Museum
National Parks Board Office
Hout St
Bree St
Church St
Townhouse
Sluttaford's
Town Square
Greenmarket Square
Longmarket St
Church St
Groote Kerk
St George's Cathedral
Parliament St
Bureau of Heraldry
Cultural History Museum
Government Printers
Corporation St
Mostert St
Spin St
Plein St
Barrack St
Longmarket St
Albertus St
Department of Home Affairs
Commercial St
Roeland St
Buitenkant St
Rust-en-Vreugd
Hope St
Glynn St
Wandel St

4

Waterkant St
Hudson
Rose St
Hout St
Berg St
Chiappini St
Strand St
Castle St
Buitengracht St
Lutheran
M62
Shortmarket St
The Virtual Turtle Internet
Riebeeck Square
Longmarket St
Bree St
African Image
Noor el Hamedia
Wale St
St George's St
Cape Nature Conservation
South African Library
Houses of Parliament
De Tuynhuys
Central
Keerom St
Queen Victoria St
Green St
Company's Gardens
Government Ave
Bouquet St
St John's St
Tuinn Plein St
Hope St La
Vrede St
Barnet St
Gallery La
National Gallery
Jewish Museum
Dunkley Square
Paddock Ave

5

Longmarket St
Carl St
August St
Church St
St
Bo-Kaap (Cape Muslim Quarter)
Hilligers St
Wale St
Bo-Kaap Museum
Dve
Dorp St
Leeuwen St
Upper Leeuwen St
Buitengracht St
Service St
Pepper St
Bloem St
Buiten St
New Church St
Bree St
Orphan St
Buitensingle St
Long St
Loop St
Long St Baths
Perth St
Greys Pass
South African Museum
Museum
Orange St
Little
Bertam House
Kloof Rd
Beckham St
Victoria St
Jamieson Rd
Carisbrook St
Dorman St
Rheede St
Faure St
Labia
M53

6

Voetboog Rd
Military Rd
Astiana St
Yusuf Rd
Schotsche Kloof
Upper Pepper St
Jordan St
Bryant St
Lion St
Upper Bloem St
Pentz St
Tamboerskloof
Lion's Rump
Whitford St
Carisbrook Rd
Peace St
Carisbrook Rd
Military Rd
Milloff Manor
Milner Rd
Hillside St
Carstens St
Tamboerskloof St
Upper Buitengracht St
New Church St
To Camps Bay
Kohling St
Park House Rd
Park La
Kloof St
Kloof St
Wilkinson St
Kloof Nek Rd
Eaton Rd
M62

E   F   G   H

For more detail around Cape Town, refer to Map 90

0   200   400 m
0   200   400 yd

A

O'Reilly
Prospect
Catherine
Banket
To Yeoville
Kapteijn
Quartz
Esselen
Germany
Twist
Edith Cavell
Kotze
Klein
Windybrow
Hadfield
Windybrow People's Market
Windybrow Centre for the Arts
To Bez Valley
Hillbrow
Claim
Smit
To Orange Grove & M1
Johannesburg Fort
Hospital
South African Institute for Medical Research
De Korte
Joubert
Civic Theatre
Loveday
Australia
Simmonds
Hoof
Biccard
Melle
Ameshoff
Alexander Theatre
Jorissen
Braamfontein
De Korte
Bertha
Station
Juta
Henri
Parktonian
Botswana
Smit
Stiemens
Devonshire
De Beer
Jan Smuts
To Northern Suburbs & M1
Mozambique Information Office
Braamfontein Centre; Swaziland Consulate
Malawi
University of Witwatersrand
Eendracht
Enoch Sontonga
Braamfontein Cemetery
Smit
For more detail around Johannesburg, refer to Map 68

B

Davies
Belt
Nugget
Banket
Bok
Koch
Leyds
Quartz
Wolmarans
King George
Saxtona
Joubert Park
Claim
Minibus Taxis to Bulawayo (Zimbabwe)
Minibus Taxis to Maputo (Mozambique)
Joubert Park
Johannesburg Art Gallery
Twist
Northern & Eastern Buses
Minibus Taxis to Pretoria
Bridge
Wanderers
Long-distance Minibus Taxis
Minibus Taxis to Upington, Kimberley & Cape Town
Site of Proposed Road Transport Interchange
Metro Concourse
Transit Centre
City to City Bus Office
Johannesburg Train Station
Proposed Retail Malls
Rissik
Smit
Leyds
Wolmarans
Simmonds
Juta
Biccard
Melle
Queen Elizabeth
De Villiers Graaff
Smit

C

End Street Park
Nugget
Mozambique
Gold
Hancock
Claim
Lesotho, Bloemfontein, Kroonstad & Ficksburg
Kwa Indaba Muti
Noord
Twist
Minibus Taxis to Soweto
De Villiers
Plein
Bree
Kerk
Mooi
Polly
Jeppe
Shell House
Klein
Minibus Taxis to Durban
Minibus Taxis to Rosebank & Sandton
St Mary's Anglican Cathedral
Smal St Mall
GPO
Supreme Court
Eloff
Bree
De Villiers
Plein
Joubert
Kerk
Loveday
Springbok
Harrison
Simmonds
Department of Home Affairs
Zimbabwe
Sauer
Diagonal
West
Carr
Pim
West
Bree
Jeppe
French Institute of South Africa
Market Theatre Complex
Museum Africa
Workers' Museum
Newtown
SA Breweries Museum
Kwa Indaba Muti
Hindu Temple
Kohinoor Music Store
Becker
Fox
President
Wolhuter
Goch
Carr
Quinn
Pim
Bree
Jeppe
Malherbe
Oriental Plaza

D

To Troyeville
Nugget
Gold
Mooi
Anderson
Market
Commissioner
Mooi
Troye
Delvers
Main
Marshall
Von Weilligh
Pritchard
President
France
Carlton Centre
Gauteng Tourism Association & AmEx
Jewish Museum
Kine Centre
USA Consulate
Kruis
Von Brandis
Eloff
Vanderbijl Square
Marshalltown
Market
Rissik St
Johannesburg
Fox
Loveday
City Hall
Soweto Art Gallery
Pritchard
Commissioner
Main
To Standard Bank Centre Gallery
Ferreira
Kort
Market
West
Becker
Fox
Magistrates Court
Bezuidenho
Wolhute
Alexande
Main
To M2 & Johannesburg International Airport
Park
Avenue
Park
Main
Pine
Fordsburg
Nursery

200   400 m
200   400 yd

INDIAN OCEAN

Bay of Plenty Beach
Bay of Plenty Pier
North Beach Pier
Dairy Beach Pier
New Pier
Seaworld
Wedge Pier
Al's Bike Hire
Erskine
Prince
Rutherford
Point

Mini Town
Snell Pde
Playfair
John McIntyre
Harris Cres
Ocean City (Theatre & Ice Rink)
Somtseu
Brickhill
Holiday Inn Garden Court
Molyneux
Pavilion Tce
Hoy Park Sports Ground

Promenade
Surfboard Hire
Marine Pde
Information Kiosk
West St Mall
Tyzack
Smith
Gillespie
Sea View
Beatty
Thistle
The Wheel
Rochester
Sturdee
Point

Boscombe
Victoria Park
Old Fort
Brickhill
Morrison
Hunter
Milne Rd
Pine
Palmer
Kearsney
Farewell
Fairport
Gull
Mazeppa
Fisher
Pickering
Winder
Bay Tce
Quayside

Prince Alfred
Stanger
Stanger
Alayam Hindu Temple
Kingsmead Cricket Ground
Walnut
Union
Commercial
West
Smith
Cato
Roy
Creek
Kitchener
Mills
Vasco da Gama
Clock

To Umhlanga Rocks & North Coast
NMR Ave
Taylor Cres
Old Fort Warriors Gate
Ordnance
Central Park
Durban Exhibition Centre
Aliwal
The Workshop
Local Bus Terminus
Medwood Gardens
Local History Museum
Cato Square
Airport Bus
The Movies
Aliwal
Albany
Acutt
Hilmark Car Rental
Embankment
Natal Maritime Museum; Boat Cruises
BAT Centre
Natal Bay

Old Fort
KwaMuhle Museum
Local Buses to Umhlanga Rocks
St Paul's
Tourist Junction
GPO
National Science Museum; Library; Art Gallery
City Hall
Royal Natal Playhouse
African Art Centre
Dick King Statue
Victoria Embankment

Durban Train Station
Long-distance Minibus Taxis
Umgeni
Soldiers Way
Pine
Field
Francis Farewell Square
Gardiner
Smith
Germany
Field
USA
UK

May
Fynn
North
Mitchell
Newmarket
Ascot
First
Umgeni
Commercial
American Express
320 Towers
AA Office
Medical Centre
Fenton
Beach
Victoria Embankment

Epsom
Albert
Beatrice
Leopold
Prince Edward
Albert
Victoria
Queen
West St
Broad

To Campbell Collections Museum
Royal Durban Golf Course
Racecourse
Dartnell Cres
Grey
Lorne
Cross
Alice
Cross
Grey
Victoria
Juma Madrassa Arcade
Victoria St Indian Market
Emmanuel Cathedral
Russell
Medical Centre
AA Office
Old House Museum
Russell
St Georges
St Andrews
Albert Park

Greyville
Sydenham Rd
Centenary
Carlisle
Bus Depot
Cross
Russell
West St Cemetery
Theatre
West
Smith
Park

To Botanic Gardens
Municipal Sports Ground
Winterton
Mansfield
Warwick
Old Dutch
Canongate
Victoria Bus Terminus
Fruit & Vegetable Market
Berea Rd
Market
Minibus Taxis
Brook
Lancers
Warwick
Minibus Taxi to Lusikisiki (Transkei)
Sydney
Alexandra

To Morningside & Mitchell Park
To South Coast & Durban (Louis Botha) Airport

For more detail around Durban, refer to Map 81

Scale 1:26,000

0   250   500 m
0   250   500 yd

A   **B**   **C**   **D**

Frederika
Gezina Square
M8
Michael Brink
M1
Gezina
H F Verwoerd
Ella
Gezina
Tenth
Thirteenth
Fourteenth

Capital Park
R101
Capital Park
Myburgh
Capital Park
Behrens
M8
Trouw
Trouw
Jacobs
Adcock
First
Second
Third
Fourth
Fifth
Sixth
Seventh
Eigth
Flowers
Van Heerden
Flowers
M8
Malherbe
Venter
M5
Malan
Union
Viljoen
Rose
Blake
Riviera

Pretoria Academic
Municipal Sports Ground
Annie Betha

National Zoological Gardens
Dr Savage
Soutpansberg

Apies
River
Canal
Paul Kruger
Belle Ombre
Soutpansberg
Dr Savage
Beatrix
Belvedere

Boom
Bloed
Long-distance Minibus Taxis
Edmond
Hamilton
Union Buildings

To North-West Province
N4
Long-distance Minibus Taxis
Struben
Paul Kruger
Proes
Vermeulen
To Foreign Embassies, Mpumalanga, Northern Province & Johannesburg

N4
Schubart
Vermeulen
JG Strijdom Square
Tourist Rendezvous Centre
Du Toit
Church (Kerk)
Church (Kerk)
Arcadia
Pretorius
N4
Wessels

Heroes' Acre Cemetery
Paul Kruger House
Bosman
Church Square
Bus Terminus
State
Dion
Sterland
Schoeman
N4
Pretoria Art Museum

Church (Kerk)
Paul Kruger
Pretoria Tourism
GPO
Pretorius
Edward
Caledonian Sports Ground
Jeppe
Park

Showgrounds
Pretorius
Police Museum
St Alban's Cathedral
Sanlam Centre
Pretoria Hof Tramshed Complex
Schoeman

Dept of Home Affairs
Skinner
To Hatfield Flea Market

Skinner
Science & Technology Museum
Andries
Van der Walt
Skinner
Sunnypark
Esselen
Metro Cine 1,2,3; Camping Centre
Pharmacy
Celliers
Esselen
Leyds
Bourke
Spuy

National Museum of Culture
Visagie
Holiday Inn Garden Court
Jubilee Square
Kotze
De Kock

Correctional Service Museum
Minnaar
Transvaal Museum of Anthropology & Geology
Burgers Park
Prinsloo
Gerhard Moerdyk
Joubert
Mears
Troye
Sunnyside
Reilly
Vos
Plein
Jorissen
M11

M1
Jacob Maré
Melrose House
Scheiding
Rissik

Barracks
Victoria
Bosman Street
Berea Park
Walker
Reitz

Dequar
Greyhound, Translux Intercape Terminal
Railway
M5
Devenish Street
M11

Soetdoring
Skietpoort
Pretoria
Andries
Berea
Mears Street
Berea
Walker Street

Salvoklop
Normaal
Elandspoort
Troye
Bourke
Leyds
Zuid Afrikaans Clinic
Muckleneuk

Klawer
R101
Mears
St Patricks
To Johannesburg International Airport (46km)
To National Parks Board (Head Office)

R28

For more detail around Pretoria, refer to Map 51

125　　250 m
125　　250 yd

E　　**F**　　**G**　　**H**

Van Praagh Ave

Coxwell Ave

wland quare

eveland Ave

Blakiston St

Beit Ave

Alexandra Sports Ground

Denmark Ave

Belgravia

To Parirenyatwa Hospital

Royal Harare Golf Club

To National Botanic Gardens

Harare Sports Club

Polo Ground

1

Josiah Tongogara Ave

Mazowe St

Second St

Third St

Fourth St

Baines Ave

Sixth St

Fife Avenue Shopping Centre

Josiah Tongogara Ave

Josiah Chinamano Ave

Josiah Chinamano Ave

Harare St

Blakiston St

Baines Ave

Tanzania

Leopold Takawira St

Colquhoun St

Canada

Prince Edward Street

Fife Ave

USA

Mozambique

Fife Ave

Herbert Chitepo Ave

2

Herbert Chitepo Ave

Sacred Heart

Livingstone Ave

Fifth St

Rainbow

Kenya

Second St

Park La

Selous Ave

Central Ave

To Mutare

3

Harare Gardens

Theatre in the Park

National Gallery of Zimbabwe

France

France

Samora Machel Ave

Third St

Holiday Inn

Les Brown Swimming Pool

Crowne Plaza

Avenues

Union Ave

Park La

Surveyor General

Karigamombe Centre

Australia; Japan

Anglican Cathedral

Parliament

To Showgrounds, National Sports entre, Heroes' Acre & Bulawayo

Germany

Samora Machel Ave

UK

Zambia

Liquenda House; Immigration

Nelson Mandela Ave

Fourth St

Ave

4

Buses for Heroes' Acre

Park St

Union Ave

Booklover's Paradise

George Silundika St

First St

Nelson

Mandela Ave

African Unity Square

Thomas Cook

Ave

ZANU Headquarters

Nelson Mandela Ave

Kingston's Bookshop

Second St

Publicity Association

Fourth St

Pennefather Ave

Zimbabwe Tourist Authority

Rezende St

GPO

Israel

Jason Moyo

Meikles

Blue Arrow Office

Zimbabwe Museum of Human Sciences

Jason Moyo Ave

Angwa St

Speke St

Trans-Lux Bus Office

New Zealand

Willoughby Cres

Chinhoyi St

Speke Ave

Julius Nyerere Way

Inez Tce

Town House

Robert Mugabe Rd

Eastgate Centre; Travellers' Info Centre

Raleigh St

Luck St

Albion Rd

Harare

Manica Cycles

Rainbow City Complex

To Coronation Park Campground, Chapungu Kraal, Epworth & Mutare

Courtauld

Robert Mugabe Rd

Chinhoyi St

Cameron St

Leopold Takawira St

Rezende St

Robson Manyika Ave

Internet Village

Wynne St

5

Rotten Row

Harare St

Mbuya Nehanda St

Bank Street

Angwa St

South Ave

Zack's Cycles

Kenneth Kaunda Ave

Harare

elvedere Rd

Kaguvi St

Market Square

Bute Street

Kopje

The Kopje

Skipper Hoste Dve

Ivan Maguire Way

Malawi

Charter Rd

Abercom St

Seke Rd

To Mbare Musika Bus Terminal

To Airport

Mukuvisi River

6

E　　**F**　　**G**　　**H**

0   250   500 m
0   250   500 yd

A   **B**   **C**   **D**

1

Windhoek State Hospital

Schoeman
Hugo
Blackett
Pullman
Osler
Ellis
Kutako Dve
Hosea

Shakespeare
Luther
France
Independence
Goethe
Robert Mugabe
Liliencron
Promenaden
Schanzen
Ossmann
Uhland

Harvey
Robert Koch
Lister
Johann Albrecht
Pettenkofer
Van Rhijn
Freud

2

Florence Nightingale
Ross
Pasteur
Pavlov
Schweitzer
Pasteur
Freud
Adler
Davey

Old Supreme Court
Kenya
Korner
Windhoek
Trans-Namib Transport Museum
Owambo Campaign Memorial
Villa Migliarina
Werth Lookout
Werth
Villa Lanvers
Schanzen
Sinclair
Hofmeyer
Bahnhof
Turnhalle
Moltke
Ave
Oode Voorpost; MET
UK
Kudu Memorial

Jenner
Salk
Willan
Schonlein
Simpson
Banting
Windhoek West

3

Curie
Roentgen
Beethoven
John Meinert
Strauss
Wagner
Brahms
Bach
Brahms
Verdi
Villa Verdi
Bülow
Rossini
Brahms
Storch
Schubert

John Meinert
Drs Rabie & Retief
Minibuses for the South
Mandume
Ministry of Home Affairs (Immigration)
National Gallery
Lüderitz
St George's Anglican Cathedral
Windhoek Public Library
Owela (State) Museum
Kasino
Roman Catholic Cathedral & Hospital
Stübel
Levinson Arcade
Bülow
New Namibia Books
GPO
Telecommunications Office
State House
Independence
Post
Windhoek Information & Publicity Office
Park
Zoo Park
Old Magistrates' Court
Old German Lutheran Church
Tintenpalast (Parliament Building)
Hauptkasse
Ndemufayo
Wernhill Park Centre
Anderson
Love

4

To Daan Viljoen Game Park
B6
Sam Nujoma Dve
Bach
Mozart
Louis Botha
Mahler
Blohm
Schuster
Bismarck
Wecke
Ave
Peter Müller
Der Bücherkeller Bookshop
Grab-a-Phone
Bus Terminal
Kalahari Sands
Kaiserliche Realschule
Christuskirche (Lutheran Church)
Alte Feste (State Museum)
Gustav Voigts Centre
Neser
Officers' House
Curt von François Monument
Hügel
To Windhoek International Airport
B6
Sam Nujoma Dve
Robert Mugabe
Schwerinsburg
Schwerinsburg
Sandpiper
Edelvalk
Eulen
Purcell
Elgar
Kutako
Hosea
Sam Nujoma
Hoogenhout
Viljoen
Church
Namibia Crafts Centre
Ave
Garten
Tal
The Warehouse

Hochland Park

5

Papageien
Egret
Barbet
Papageien
Goshawk
Liszt
Kerby
Bismarck
Nachtigal
Schmerenbeck
Haddy
Mandume
Ndemufayo Ave
Trift
Schinz
Merensky
Trift
Church
Rehobother
Angola
Ausspannplatz
Guthenberg
Macadam
Feld
Jan
Lossen
Lazarett
Heinitzburg
Heinitzburg
Sanderbur
Ave
Burg
Chateau
Schwerinsburg
Sperlingslust
Heinitzburg

6

Windhoek Crematorium & Cemetery
Gammams
Marconi
Planck
Von Braun
Voigts
Edison
Keppler
Hochland
Bell
Lazarett
Campbell
Patterson
Armstrong
Stoke
Bell
Faraday
Galilei
Jonker
Intercape Mainliner Office
Newton
Feld
Ballot
Thore
Centaurus
Maerua Park Centre

A   **B**   **C**   **D**

For more detail around Windhoek, refer to Map 39

250   500 m
250   500 yd

To Metro Mall

Bosele

To Airport (6km) & Francistown (440km)

Broadhurst

Serotelakgamelo

To Gaborone Game Reserve

Mohatha Rd

Segoditshane River

Segoditshane

To Broadhurst North Mall

Lekakauwe

Limpopo Dve

Francistown Road

Potsana

Kolobe

Middle Star (Julius Nyerere)

Sebalabolokwane

Ntseane

Segogwane
Maru-a-Pula (No Mathatha)

Julius Nyerere Dve

Metsemasweu Rd

Maitisong Cultural Centre

To Mt Kgale, Mokolodi Nature Reserve & St Clair Lion Park

Western Bypass

Madibeng

Elephant

Maruapula

Marakanelo

Sobhuza

Tshekedi

Tshekedi

Zebra

Phuti

th Commercial

Nelson Mandela Dve

Independence Ave

Kgalagadi

President's Dve

Nswazwi

Moremi

Buffalo

Phiri Cres

Julius Nyerere Dve

Gaborone Sun

Golf Course

Eastern Commercial St

State House

Kalahari Conservation Society

North Ring Rd

Hospital Way

Phala

National Stadium

Department of Immigration

National Parks Office

Cres

Air Botswana

Botswana Book Centre

National Museum & Art Gallery

Princess Marina Hospital

Visa Extensions

National Assembly

Queensway

Pula

The Mall

Tourist Office

Notwane Rd

o Mogoditshane

lepolole
Bus
erminal

USA

Khama

UK

GPO

Botswana Rd

Circle

Church

University of Botswana

Former BDF Airport

Molepolole Flyover

State House Dve

Botsalano (Debswana) House

France

Mathangwane

Kabelo

Alliance Française

Mobutu Dve

Metsemo Ithaba

Shashe Rd Nth

Gaborone

Botswana Telecom

Orapa House

Mogonono

African Mall

South Ring Rd

Jawara Rd

Gaborone Club

Market

tation

Makolwane

Kenneth Kaunda Rd

Moeding

Bushbuck

Oodi

Maratadiba Rd

Phuthadikobo

Village Mall & Cinema

National Botanical Garden & Natural History Centre

Mmupudu

Independence Ave

Tholo

Pitse

Flamingo

Giraffe

Kwatsi

Hippopotamus

Oodi

Boteti

The Village

Shashe Rd Sth

Haile Salassie

Old Lobatse Rd

Mokotedi

Malope

Willoughby

Bontleng

Allison Cres

Botswana Polytechnic

Tlokweng Rd

Ngotwane River

ew Lobatse Rd

Dve

Machel

Showgrounds

Samora
Cresta Lodge

0   250   500 m
0   250   500 yd

A   **B**   **C**   **D**

Baia de Maputo

1

Avenida do Zimbabwe
Arcebispado
Sommerchield
Praça do Destacamento Femminio
To Costa do Sol
Praça do
Artedif Crafts
Eduardo Mondlane University

2

Presidentes
Avenida Kenneth Kaunda
Avenida Zambia
Cahora Bassa
Clínica de Sommerchield
Gen Teixeira Botelho
Pero de Anaia
Mãe e Vascorados Água
Tchamba
Francisco Barreto
Avenida Kim II Sung
Germany
USA
Malawi
Joao de Barros
Santo António da Polana
Local Bus Stop
Nyerere
Polana
Canada
Marginal
Avenida Julius
Fontes Pereira
Panthera Azul (Bus) Office
US Information Service
Zimbabwe
Pharmacy
Parque dos Continuadores
Swaziland
Netherlands
Tivane
South Africa
Panthera Azul (Bus) Office
Friedrich Engels
Avenida Martires da Machava
Avenida Tomas Nduda
Avenida Armando
Avenida Francisco Magumbe
Tanzania
Public Information Bureau (PIB)
Praça do OMM
Avenida Bassa N'Tchinga
Central Hospital
Transport Stand
Rua da Base N'Tchinga

3

Rua Malhangalene
Rua da Resistência
Rua da Resistência
Nambu Productions
Market
Avenida Vladimir Lenine
Avenida Mao Tse Tung
Avenida Kwame Nkrumah
Paulo Samuel Kankhomba
Avenida Agostinho Neto
Avenida Salvador Allende
Avenida Amilcar Cabral
Avenida Ahmed
Interfranca
Avenida Sekou Touré
Avenida 24 de Julho
Avenida Patrice Lumumba
Praça Travessia de Zambeze
Connection Time Internet Café
Geology Museum
Natural History Museum
Rua da Argelia
Rua José Mateus
Avenida José Mateus
Avenida Lusiadas
Rua da Muthemba
Rua de Nachingwea
Rua de Mueda
Avenida Martines de Cardoso
Campo do Desportivo
Avenida Olof Palme

4

Milagre Mabore
Avenida Acordos de Lusaka
Praça 20 de Setembro
Avenida Emilia Dausse
Ronil Maguiguana Transport Stop
Avenida de Angola
Avenida Eduardo Mondlane
Avenida Karl Marx
Guerra Popular
City Hall
Cathedral
Rovuma-Carlton
Centro Cultural Franco-Moçambicano
UK
Radio Clube
Botanic Gardens
National Library
33 Storey Building
ENT (National Tourism Organisation)
Centro do Desportivo
Avenida 25 de Setembro
Avenida 10 de Novembro
Avenida de Timor Leste

5

Malhangalene
Avenida Marian N'Gouabi
Praça 21 de Outubro
Irmaos Roby
To Airport
Estacio Dias
Avenida da Zambia
Avenida Lucas Luali
Avenida Albert Luthuli
Avenida Fernandes Farinha
Avenida Mohamed Said Barre
Avenida Filipe Samuel Magaia
Avenida Josina Machel
Avenida Ho Chi Min
Museum of the Revolution
Casa de Cultura
Avenida da Guerra Popular
Alto Maé
National Art Museum
Praça da Independência
Casa de Ferro
Madal
Samora Machel
Teatro Avenida
Avenida 25 de Junho
Praça 25 de Junho
Fort
Municipal Market
Taxis & Local Buses
Rua de Bagamoyo
Rua de Pedroso
Money Museum
Avenida Fernão de Magalhães
Avenida Zedequias Manganhela

6

Avenida do Trabalho
Avenida da Tanzania
Rua do Rio Tembe
Rua Paiva Couceiro
Avenida 24 de Julho
Rua do Limpopo
Avenida do Rio Limpopo
Rua Com Baeta Neves
Rua do Malanga
To Oliviera's Bus Depot
Estancias
Laurentina Beer Factory & Transport for Swaziland, South Africa, Namaacha, Boane & Goba
Paulino Santos Gil
Avenida 25 de Setembro
Praça dos Trabalhadores
Maputo
Port
Rio Espiritu Santo
Ferry to Catembe & Chapa to Ponta d'Ouro
Catembe

For more detail around Maputo, refer to Map 71

0.5   1 km
0.25   0.5 mi

E   **F**   **G**   **H**

University of Zambia

To Airport, Chipata & South Luangwa National Park

Showgrounds

Polo Field

Manda Hill Shopping Centre

Manda Hill

Great East Rd

Sibweni Rd

Chitemene Rd

Nangwenya Rd

Lukasa Rd

Lubu Rd

Chaholi

Public Swimming Pool

Lusaka Sports Club

Lusaka City

Golf Course

Los Angeles Blvd

Presidents La

Army Barracks

Zimbabwe Ave

Halle Selassie Ave

InterContinental

Tanzania
Canada
Kenya
Kenyatta

Botswana
'Diplomatic Triangle'
Netherlands
UK & USA
UN

Ridgeway

Chisidza Cres

Ngumbo Rd

Independence Ave

Nsumbu
Ngulube

Manekela

Nationalist Rd

University Teaching Hospital

Bande Rd

Paul

Jacaranda Rd

Government

Government Area (Ministries)

Kabwata Cultural Centre

Kabwata

Namibia
Kabanga
Salse
Nalubutu
Mushemi
Kasisi

Ababa Ave

Chipovu

Mambulima

Lagos

Katemo

Tito

Los Angeles Blvd

Chikwa Rd

Addis

Padmodzi
Suez Rd

Chimanga

Mogadishu

Birdcage Walk

Mwenya Rd

Lubwa Rd

Lusaka Playhouse

Holiday Inn

Kombe Rd

Nsunzu Rd

Burma Rd

Mopani Rd
Zimba Rd
Indus

Malata

Chiwa Rd

Chikonkoto

Manchichi Rd

Limbe Rd

Paseli Rd

Benakale

Nchenja

Chozi

Lubambe Rd

Mozambique

Northmead Shopping Centre & Market

Kapila

Omelo Rd

Fairview Medical Centre

Mwilwa Rd

Bwinjimfumo Rd

Parirenyetwa Rd

Democratic Republic of Congo (Zaire)

Lubuto

Church Rd

Ituna
Chilubi
Muchisha

Dushambe

Independence Ave

Changa

Gandhi

Metropolitan Sports Club

Obote Rd

Chillumbuli Rd

Mkushi

Luapula

Mvualie

Great East Rd

Provident

Makishi Rd

Kabelenga

Broads Rd

Rd

Busi.Net

Nasser

National Museum

TAZARA House & ZNIB House

Karnwala Market

Bombay Rd

To Ndola, Kitwe & Democratic Republic of Congo (Zaire)

Mukosa Rd

Makishi

Wamulwa

North End Roundabout

Great North Rd

Chandwe Musonda Rd

Musonda-Ngosa Rd

Mwayi Rd

Nchoncho Rd

Kutwa

Luanshya

Panganini

Zintu Shop

Kalambo Rd

Lumumba Rd

RPS

Chachacha Rd

Freedom Way

To Mumbwa & Kafue National Park

Kalundwe Rd

Lumumba Rd

Sadzu Rd

Dedan Kimathi Rd

Cairo Rd

The Book House

GPO

British Council

Sapele

Town Centre Market

Chiparamba

Pharmacy

Nkwazi

Katondo

Katunjila

Kulima Towers City Bus Station

Los Angeles Rd

Minibus Station

Soweto Market

Ben Bella Rd

Kolando Rd

Intercity Bus Station

Memado House; Australia

Euro-Africa Bus Station

South End Roundabout

Comesa Building

To Castle Shopping Centre, Kafue, Chirundu & Livingstone

Kafue Rd

For more detail around Lusaka, refer to Map 18

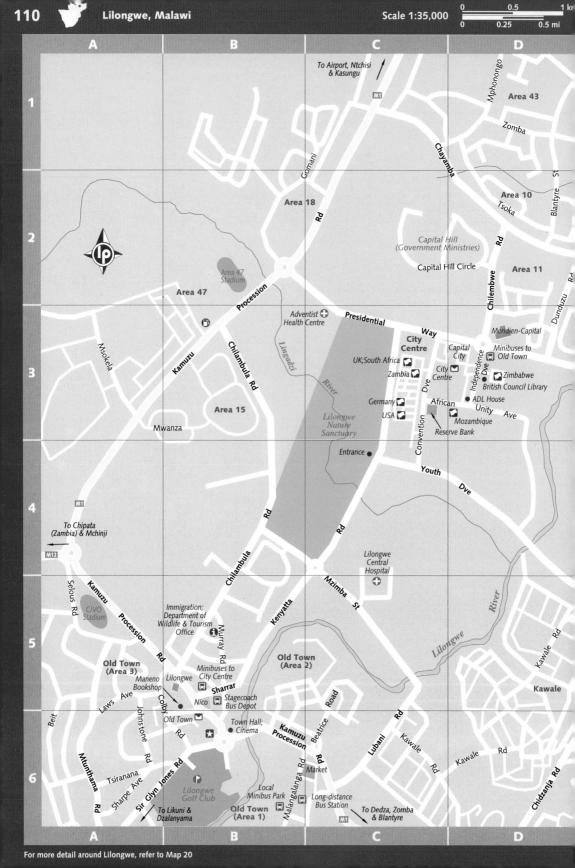

125   250 m
125   250 yd

Malunge

Mphakatsi

North

Mathews

Fitz

Mission

Allister Miller

Golf Club

Fiddes

Lanham

*Prince of
Wales Park*

Polinjane

Lidwala

Edwards

Muir

Hill

*Coronation
Park*

Mbabane
● Club

Schoch

The Avenue

Information
Office

Swaziland
Theatre Club

Polinjane

Luvatsi

Gilfillan

Morris

Indingilizi
Gallery

Polinjane River

Mhlonhlo

Hill

Howe

Twist

Omni
Centre

Allister Miller

Post

Market

Mhlonhlo

Shield

Smuts

Johnson

Bert

Church

Walker   (Mhlonhlo)

Germany

Msunduza

Ungwembe

City Inn

Tin

Msunduza

Riverside Dve

West

OK Rd

Western

Minibus Taxi Park;
Bus Station

Warner   (Msunduza)

Madwaleni

Riverside
Cres

Mbabane   River

The Mall

Swazi
Market

Jekwa

South
Africa

Swazi
Plaza

Commercial

Distributor

Southern   Distributor

Sheffield

Mbabane   River

Jojo

To Oshoek
Border Post) (21km)
& Badplaas (74km)

Tourist
Office

Ilunga

Vunte

Isomi

Mswili

Gule

Mbabane

To Oshoek
order Post) (22km)
Badplass (75km)

Bypass

Umlilo

Coventry Cres

Mlambanyatsi

Lusutfu Rd

Mbabane
Hospital

Siteshi

Stores

City to City
Bus Station

Government
Offices

To Mhlambanyatsi
(27km)

Lusutfu   Rd

To Mozambique Embassy,
Ezulwini Valley (18km),
Manzini (32km)

LONELY PLANET

MAPS & ATLASES

Lonely Planet's City Maps feature downtown and metropolitan maps as well as public transport routes and walking tours. The maps come with a complete index of streets and sights and a plastic coat for extra durability.

Road Atlases are an essential navigation tool for serious travellers. Cross-referenced with the guidebooks, they feature distance and climate charts and a comprehensive index.

Amsterdam City Map
ISBN 1 86450 081 6
US$5.95 • UK£3.99 • 39FF

Bangkok City Map
ISBN 1 86450 004 2
US$5.95 • UK£3.99 • 39FF

Barcelona City Map
ISBN 1 86450 174 X
US$5.95 • UK£3.99 • 39FF

Beijing City Map
ISBN 1 86450 255 X
US$5.95 • UK£3.99 • 39FF

Berlin City Map
ISBN 1 86450 005 0
US$5.95 • UK£3.99 • 39FF

Boston City Map
ISBN 1 86450 175 8
US$5.95 • UK£3.99 • 39FF

Brussels City Map
ISBN 1 86450 256 8
US$5.95 • UK£3.99 • 39FF

Budapest City Map
ISBN 1 86450 077 8
US$5.95 • UK£3.99 • 39FF

Cairo City Map
ISBN 1 86450 257 6
US$5.95 • UK£3.99 • 39FF

Cape Town City Map
ISBN 1 86450 076 X
US$5.95 • UK£3.99 • 39FF

Chicago City Map
ISBN 1 86450 006 9
US$5.95 • UK£3.99 • 39FF

Dublin City Map
ISBN 1 86450 176 6
US$5.95 • UK£3.99 • 39FF

Hong Kong City Map
ISBN 1 86450 007 7
US$5.95 • UK£3.99 • 39FF

Istanbul City Map
ISBN 1 86450 080 8
US$5.95 • UK£3.99 • 39FF

Jerusalem City Map
ISBN 1 86450 096 4
US$5.95 • UK£3.99 • 39FF

London City Map
ISBN 1 86450 008 5
US$5.95 • UK£3.99 • 39FF

Los Angeles City Map
ISBN 1 86450 258 4
US$5.95 • UK£3.99 • 39FF

Melbourne City Map
ISBN 1 86450 009 3
US$5.95 • UK£3.99 • 39FF

Miami City Map
ISBN 1 86450 177 4
US$5.95 • UK£3.99 • 39FF

New York City City Map
ISBN 1 86450 010 7
US$5.95 • UK£3.99 • 39FF

Paris City Map
ISBN 1 86450 011 5
US$5.95 • UK£3.99 • 39FF

Prague City Map
ISBN 1 86450 012 3
US$5.95 • UK£3.99 • 39FF

Rio de Janeiro City Map
ISBN 1 86450 013 1
US$5.95 • UK£3.99 • 39FF

Rome City Map
ISBN 1 86450 259 2
US$5.95 • UK£3.99 • 39FF

San Francisco City Map
ISBN 1 86450 014 X
US$5.95 • UK£3.99 • 39FF

Singapore City Map
ISBN 1 86450 178 2
US$5.95 • UK£3.99 • 39FF

St Petersburg City Map
ISBN 1 86450 179 0
US$5.95 • UK£3.99 • 39FF

Sydney City Map
ISBN 1 86450 015 8
US$5.95 • UK£3.99 • 39FF

Washington, DC City Map
ISBN 1 86450 078 6
US$5.95 • UK£3.99 • 39FF

Australia Road Atlas
ISBN 1 86450 065 4
US$14.99 • UK£8.99 • 109FF

Southern Africa Road Atlas
ISBN 1 86450 101 4
US$14.99 • UK£8.99 • 109FF

Thailand, Vietnam, Laos & Cambodia Road Atlas
ISBN 1 86450 102 2
US$14.99 • UK£8.99 • 109FF

Available wherever books are sold

LONELY PLANET

You already know that Lonely Planet produces more than this one road atlas, but you might not be aware of the other products we have on this region. Here is a selection of titles that you may want to check out as well:

Southern Africa
ISBN 0 86442 662 3
US$27.99 • UK£16.99 • 189FF

Africa on a shoestring
ISBN 0 86442 663 1
US$29.99 • UK£17.99 • 199FF

Malawi
ISBN 1 86450 095 6
US$17.99 • UK£11.99 • 139FF

Mozambique
ISBN 1 86450 108 1
US$19.99 • UK£11.99 • 139FF

South Africa, Lesotho & Swaziland
ISBN 0 86442 757 3
US$21.95 • UK£13.99 • 170FF

Zimbabwe, Botswana & Namibia
ISBN 0 86442 545 7
US$24.95 • UK£13.99 • 170FF

Cape Town
ISBN 0 86442 485 X
US$12.95 • UK£7.99 • 100FF

Cape Town City Map
ISBN 1 86450 076 X
US$5.95 • UK£3.99 • 39FF

Read This First: Africa
ISBN 1 86450 066 2
US$14.95 • UK£8.99 • 99FF

Healthy Travel Africa
ISBN 1 86450 050 6
US$5.95 • UK£3.99 • 39FF

Watching Wildlife Southern Africa
ISBN 1 86450 035 2
US$19.99 • UK£12.99 • 149FF

Songs to an African Sunset: A Zimbabwean Story
ISBN 0 86442 472 8
US$10.95 • UK£6.99 • 90FF

LONELY PLANET

GUIDES BY REGION

L onely Planet is known worldwide for publishing practical, reliable and no-nonsense travel information in our guides and on our Web site. The Lonely Planet list covers just about every accessible part of the world. Currently there are 16 series: Travel guides, Shoestring guides, Condensed guides, Phrasebooks, Read This First, Healthy Travel, Walking guides, Cycling guides, Watching Wildlife guides, Pisces Diving & Snorkeling guides, City Maps, Road Atlases, Out to Eat, World Food, Journeys travel literature and Pictorials.

AFRICA Africa on a shoestring • Cairo • Cape Town • Cape Town City Map • East Africa • Egypt • Egyptian Arabic phrasebook • Ethiopia, Eritrea & Djibouti • Ethiopian (Amharic) phrasebook • The Gambia & Senegal • Healthy Travel Africa • Kenya • Malawi • Morocco • Moroccan Arabic phrasebook • Mozambique • Read This First: Africa • South Africa, Lesotho & Swaziland • Southern Africa • Southern Africa Road Atlas • Swahili phrasebook • Tanzania, Zanzibar & Pemba • Trekking in East Africa • Tunisia • Watching Wildlife East Africa • Watching Wildlife Southern Africa • West Africa • World Food Morocco • Zimbabwe, Botswana & Namibia

Travel Literature: Mali Blues: Traveling to an African Beat • The Rainbird: A Central African Journey • Songs to an African Sunset: A Zimbabwean Story

AUSTRALIA & THE PACIFIC Auckland • Australia • Australian phrasebook • Australia Road Atlas • Bushwalking in Australia • Cycling New Zealand • Fiji • Fijian phrasebook • Healthy Travel Australia, NZ and the Pacific • Islands of Australia's Great Barrier Reef • Melbourne • Melbourne City Map • Micronesia • New Caledonia • New South Wales & the ACT • New Zealand • Northern Territory • Outback Australia • Out to Eat – Melbourne • Out to Eat – Sydney • Papua New Guinea • Pidgin phrasebook • Queensland • Rarotonga & the Cook Islands • Samoa • Solomon Islands • South Australia • South Pacific • South Pacific phrasebook • Sydney • Sydney City Map • Sydney Condensed • Tahiti & French Polynesia • Tasmania • Tonga • Tramping in New Zealand • Vanuatu • Victoria • Watching Wildlife Australia • Western Australia

Travel Literature: Islands in the Clouds: Travels in the Highlands of New Guinea • Kiwi Tracks: A New Zealand Journey • Sean & David's Long Drive

CENTRAL AMERICA & THE CARIBBEAN Bahamas, Turks & Caicos • Baja California • Bermuda • Central America on a shoestring • Costa Rica • Costa Rica Spanish phrasebook • Cuba • Dominican Republic & Haiti • Eastern Caribbean • Guatemala • Guatemala, Belize & Yucatán: La Ruta Maya • Healthy Travel Central & South America • Jamaica • Mexico • Mexico City • Panama • Puerto Rico • Read This First: Central & South America • World Food Mexico • Yucatán

Travel Literature: Green Dreams: Travels in Central America

EUROPE Amsterdam • Amsterdam City Map • Amsterdam Condensed • Andalucía • Austria • Baltic States phrasebook • Barcelona • Barcelona City Map • Berlin • Berlin City Map • Britain • British phrasebook • Brussels, Bruges & Antwerp • Budapest • Budapest City Map • Canary Islands • Central Europe • Central Europe phrasebook • Corfu & the Ionians • Corsica • Crete • Crete Condensed • Croatia • Cycling Britain • Cycling France • Cyprus • Czech & Slovak Republics • Denmark • Dublin • Dublin City Map • Eastern Europe • Eastern Europe phrasebook • Edinburgh • Estonia, Latvia & Lithuania • Europe on a shoestring • Finland • Florence • France • Frankfurt Condensed • French phrasebook • Georgia, Armenia & Azerbaijan • Germany • German phrasebook • Greece • Greek Islands • Greek phrasebook • Hungary • Iceland, Greenland & the Faroe Islands • Ireland • Istanbul • Italian phrasebook • Italy • Krakow • Lisbon • The Loire • London • London City Map • London Condensed • Madrid • Malta • Mediterranean Europe • Mediterranean Europe phrasebook • Moscow • Munich • Norway • Out to Eat – London • Paris • Paris City Map • Paris Condensed • Poland • Portugal • Portuguese phrasebook • Prague • Prague City Map • Provence & the Côte d'Azur • Read This First: Europe • Romania & Moldova • Rome • Russia, Ukraine & Belarus • Russian phrasebook • Scandinavian & Baltic Europe • Scandinavian Europe phrasebook • Scotland • Sicily • Slovenia • South-West France • Spain • Spanish phrasebook • St Petersburg • St Petersburg City Map • Sweden • Switzerland • Trekking in Spain • Tuscany • Ukrainian phrasebook • Venice • Vienna • Walking in Britain • Walking in France • Walking in Ireland • Walking in Italy • Walking in Spain • Walking in Switzerland • Western Europe • Western Europe phrasebook • World Food France • World Food Ireland • World Food Italy • World Food Spain

Travel Literature: Love and War in the Apennines • The Olive Grove: Travels in Greece • On the Shores of the Mediterranean • Round Ireland in Low Gear • A Small Place in Italy

INDIAN SUBCONTINENT Bangladesh • Bengali phrasebook • Bhutan • Delhi • Goa • Healthy Travel Asia & India • Hindi & Urdu phrasebook • India • Indian Himalaya • Karakoram Highway • Kerala • Mumbai (Bombay) • Nepal • Nepali phrasebook • Pakistan • Rajasthan • Read This First: Asia & India • South India • Sri Lanka • Sri Lanka phrasebook • Tibet • Tibetan phrasebook • Trekking in the Indian Himalaya • Trekking in the Karakoram & Hindukush • Trekking in the Nepal Himalaya

Travel Literature: The Age of Kali: Indian Travels and Encounters • Hello Goodnight: A Life of Goa • In Rajasthan • A Season in Heaven: True Tales from the Road to Kathmandu • Shopping for Buddhas • A Short Walk in the Hindu Kush • Slowly Down the Ganges

LONELY PLANET

MAIL ORDER

Lonely Planet products are distributed worldwide. They are also available by mail order from Lonely Planet, so if you have difficulty finding a title please write to us. North and South American residents should write to 150 Linden St, Oakland, CA 94607, USA; European and African residents should write to 10a Spring Place, London NW5 3BH, UK; and residents of other countries to Locked Bag 1, Footscray, Victoria 3011, Australia.

ISLANDS OF THE INDIAN OCEAN Madagascar & Comoros • Maldives • Mauritius, Réunion & Seychelles

MIDDLE EAST & CENTRAL ASIA Bahrain, Kuwait & Qatar • Central Asia • Central Asia phrasebook • Dubai • Hebrew phrasebook • Iran • Israel & the Palestinian Territories • Istanbul • Istanbul City Map • Istanbul to Cairo on a shoestring • Jerusalem • Jerusalem City Map • Jordan • Lebanon • Middle East • Oman & the United Arab Emirates • Syria • Turkey • Turkish phrasebook • World Food Turkey • Yemen

Travel Literature: Black on Black: Iran Revisited • The Gates of Damascus • Kingdom of the Film Stars: Journey into Jordan

NORTH AMERICA Alaska • Boston • Boston City Map • California & Nevada • California Condensed • Canada • Chicago • Chicago City Map • Deep South • Florida • Hawaii • Hiking in Alaska • Hiking in the USA • Honolulu • Las Vegas • Los Angeles • Miami • Miami City Map • New England • New Orleans • New York City • New York City City Map • New York City Condensed • New York, New Jersey & Pennsylvania • Oahu • Out to Eat — San Francisco • Pacific Northwest • Puerto Rico • Rocky Mountains • San Francisco • San Francisco City Map • Seattle • Southwest • Texas • USA • USA phrasebook • Vancouver • Virginia & the Capital Region • Washington, DC City Map • World Food Deep South, USA

Travel Literature: Caught Inside: A Surfer's Year on the California Coast • Drive Thru America

NORTH-EAST ASIA Beijing • Cantonese phrasebook • China • Hiking in Japan • Hong Kong • Hong Kong City Map • Hong Kong Condensed • Hong Kong, Macau & Guangzhou • Japan • Japanese phrasebook • Korea • Korean phrasebook • Kyoto • Mandarin phrasebook • Mongolia • Mongolian phrasebook • Seoul • South-West China • Taiwan • Tokyo

Travel Literature: In Xanadu: A Quest • Lost Japan

SOUTH AMERICA Argentina, Uruguay & Paraguay • Bolivia • Brazil • Brazilian phrasebook • Buenos Aires • Chile & Easter Island • Colombia • Ecuador & the Galapagos Islands • Healthy Travel Central & South America • Latin American Spanish phrasebook • Peru • Quechua phrasebook • Read This First: Central & South America • Rio de Janeiro • Rio de Janeiro City Map • Santiago • South America on a shoestring • Trekking in the Patagonian Andes • Venezuela

Travel Literature: Full Circle: A South American Journey

SOUTH-EAST ASIA Bali & Lombok • Bangkok • Bangkok City Map • Burmese phrasebook • Cambodia • Hanoi • Healthy Travel Asia & India • Hill Tribes phrasebook • Ho Chi Minh City • Indonesia • Indonesian phrasebook • Indonesia's Eastern Islands • Jakarta • Java • Lao phrasebook • Laos • Malay phrasebook • Malaysia, Singapore & Brunei • Myanmar (Burma) • Philippines • Pilipino (Tagalog) phrasebook • Read This First: Asia & India • Singapore • Singapore City Map • South-East Asia on a shoestring • South-East Asia phrasebook • Thailand • Thailand's Islands & Beaches • Thailand, Vietnam, Laos & Cambodia Road Atlas • Thai phrasebook • Vietnam • Vietnamese phrasebook • World Food Thailand • World Food Vietnam

---

ALSO AVAILABLE: Antarctica • The Arctic • The Blue Man: Tales of Travel, Love and Coffee • Brief Encounters: Stories of Love, Sex & Travel • Chasing Rickshaws • The Last Grain Race • Lonely Planet Unpacked • Not the Only Planet: Science Fiction Travel Stories • On the Edge: Extreme Travel • Sacred India • Travel with Children • Travel Photography: A Guide to Taking Better Pictures

baia . . . . .bay	Portuguese	
barragem . . . . . .dam	Portuguese	
berg(e) . . . . . . .mountain(s)	Afrikaans	
brug . . . . .bridge	Afrikaans	
bucht . . . . .bay	Afrikaans	
burg . . . . .town	Afrikaans	
bushveld . . . . . . .bushland	Afrikaans	
cabo . . . . .cape	Portuguese	
dam . . . . .reservoir	Afrikaans	
dorp . . . . .rural settlement where road crosses a river	Afrikaans	
highveld . . . . . . .highlands	Afrikaans	
ilha . . . . .island	Portuguese
kloof . . . . .ravine or small valley	Afrikaans
kop/kopje/koppie little hill, usually flat topped	Afrikaans
lac . . . . .lake	French
lago . . . . .lake	Portuguese
lowveld . . . . . . .lowlands	Afrikaans
monte . . . . .mount	Portuguese
monts . . . . .mountains	French
nek . . . . .pass	Afrikaans
pas . . . . .pass	Afrikaans
planalto . . . . . . .plateau	Portuguese

plato . . . . .plateau — Afrikaans
ponta . . . . .point — Portuguese
poort . . . . .pass — Afrikaans
portagem . . . . . .toll road — Portuguese
porto . . . . .port — Portuguese
praia . . . . .beach — Portuguese
rio . . . . .river — Portuguese
rivier . . . . .river — Afrikaans
rivière . . . . .river — French
rua . . . . .road, street — Portuguese
sandveld . . . . . .desert — Afrikaans
serra . . . . .mountain, mountain range — Portuguese

spruit . . . . .shallow river — Afrikaans
stad . . . . .city centre — Afrikaans
strand . . . . .beach — Afrikaans
thaba . . . . .mountain — Sesotho
tswaing . . . . . . .salt pan — Tswana
veld . . . . .open grassland — Afrikaans
vila . . . . .town — Portuguese
vlei . . . . .any low open landscape, often marshy — Afrikaans
weg . . . . .street, road — Afrikaans

Abbreviations used in this index

Countries:
Angola . . . . .ANG
Botswana . . . . .BOT
Dem Rep of Congo (Zaïre) . . .DRC
Lesotho . . . . .LES
Malawi . . . . .MAL
Mozambique . . . . .MOZ
Namibia . . . . .NAM
South Africa . . . . .SAF
Swaziland . . . . .SWA
Tanzania . . . . .TAN
Zambia . . . . .ZAM
Zimbabwe . . . . .ZIM

Provinces:
Berea (LES) . . . . .Bere
Cabo Delgado (MOZ) . . . . . . .CaDe
Central Province (MAL) . . . . .CPM
Central Province (ZAM) . . . . .CPZa
Chobe (BOT) . . . . .Chob
Eastern Cape (SAF) . . . . . . .Ecap
Eastern Province (ZAM) . . . . .EPZa
Free State (SAF) . . . . .FrSt
Gauteng (SAF) . . . . .Gaut
Gaza (MOZ) . . . . .Gaza
Hardap (NAM) . . . . .Hard
Karas (NAM) . . . . .Kara

Kunene (NAM) . . . . .Kune
KwaZulu-Natal (SAF) . . . . . .KZNa
Luapula (ZAM) . . . . .Luap
Mashonaland North (ZIM) . . .MaNo
Mashonaland West (ZIM) . . . .MaWe
Mpumalanga (SAF) . . . . . . .Mpum
Nampula (MOZ) . . . . .Namp
Niassa (MOZ) . . . . .Nias
Northern Cape (SAF) . . . . . .Ncap
Northern Province (SAF) . . . .NPSA
Northern Province (ZAM) . . . .NPZa
North-West Province (SAF) . . .NWSA

Otjozondjupa (NAM) . . . . . . .Otjo
Southern Province (MAL) . . . .SPM
Southern Province (ZAM) . . . .SPZa
Tete (MOZ) . . . . .Tete
Thaba-Tseka (LES) . . . . .ThTs
Western Cape (SAF) . . . . . . .Wcap
Western Province (ZAM) . . . . .WPZa

Index